LACROSSE

Fundamentals for Winning

Sports Illustrated Winner's Circle Books

BOOKS ON TEAM SPORTS

Baseball
Football: Winning Defense
Football: Winning Offense
Hockey
Lacrosse
Pitching

BOOKS ON INDIVIDUAL SPORTS

Bowling
Competitive Swimming
Golf
Racquetball
Skiing
Tennis
Track: Championship Running

SPECIAL BOOKS

Canoeing
Fly Fishing
Scuba Diving
Strength Training

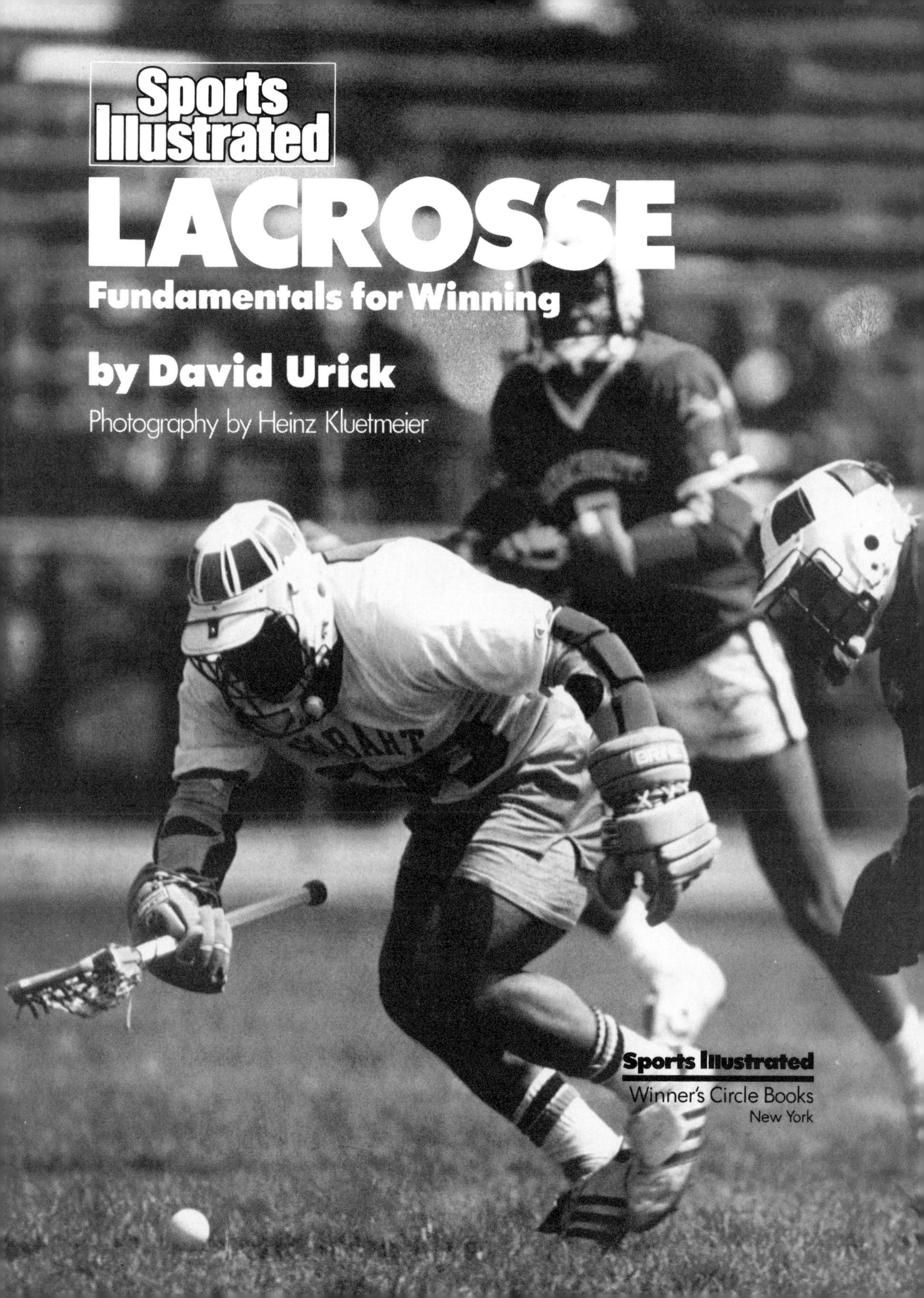

Sports Illustrated
LACROSSE
Fundamentals for Winning

by David Urick

Photography by Heinz Kluetmeier

Sports Illustrated
Winner's Circle Books
New York

To Jerry Schmidt, former lacrosse coach at Hobart College, for a willingness to share not only his great knowledge of the game but also his wonderful approach to people.

To Hobart assistant coaches Tom Korn, Terry Corcoran, Hank Janczyk, B.J. O'Hara, Pete Gillotte, Jack McDonald, and Mark VanArsdale, from whom I have learned and continue to learn so much.

To Hobart College lacrosse players, past and present, for their approach to the game—intense, proud, yet fun.

To Mrs. Dorothy DeBacco for being a fine secretary and able to read my handwriting.

To Bill Jaspersohn, editor, Sports Illustrated Winner's Circle Books, for his patience, encouragement, and expertise—particularly his patience.

To Linda Urick, for being my typist, proofreader, critic, advisor, and, most important, my best friend.

To Holly, Scott, and Mindy, for always giving their dad a good reason to smile.

And an extra-special thanks to Mom, Dad, and Linda.

Picture credits: Page 3 by Art Foxall; 10 courtesy of the Lacrosse Hall of Fame Archives; 32 by Bill Jaspersohn; 234 by Jan Regan; 26, 29, 37 (right), 50, 93, 166, 178, 220, 232, 250 by Jack Phillips. All diagrams by Frank Ronan. All other photographs by Heinz Kluetmeier.

FIRST EDITION

Designer: Kim Llewellyn

Library of Congress Cataloging-in-Publication Data

Urick, David.
     Sports illustrated lacrosse / by David Urick; photography by Heinz Kluetmeier.
          p.   cm.
     1. Lacrosse.   I. Kluetmeier, Heinz.   II. Sports illustrated (Time, inc.)   III. Title.
IV. Title: Lacrosse.
GV989.U75 1988
796.34'7—dc19   87-36462
ISBN 0-452-26043-4 (pbk.) 88 89 90 91 92 AG/HL 10 9 8 7 6 5 4 3 2 1

Contents

5

4 | Individual Defense   79

5 | Team Offense   95

6 | Extra-Man Offense   127

7 | Team Defense   141

LACROSSE

Fundamentals for Winning

Preface

Some years ago, the famed sportswriter, Grantland Rice, wrote of lacrosse:

"Once in a while they argue about the fastest game—hockey or basketball; then about the roughest game—boxing, football, or water polo. But when it comes to the top combination the answer is lacrosse, the all star combination of speed and body contact. It requires more elements of skill than any game I know."

The sport of lacrosse, the oldest-known athletic game played in North America, was originally not a sport at all. Called "baggataway" by the North American Indian tribes that founded and played it long before Columbus discovered the New World, lacrosse originated as a ceremonial religious rite. Virtually all tribes of southern Canada and the United States, except those in the Southwest, played some type of lacrosse, and games were usually preceded by solemn rituals and dances.

White settlers in the early 17th century gave lacrosse its European name. French Jesuit missionaries felt that the stick used in the contest resembled the type of staff, or crosier, carried by their bishops and known, in French, as *la crosse*. From then on, baggataway went by the name lacrosse.

The original equipment used by Indian tribes was quite simple. The lacrosse stick was a wooden shaft, curved at the top, with leather netting woven into the curved section and used for catching and throwing a ball. Materials used for balls included rocks wrapped in animal skins; carved, rounded pieces of wood, or other available round items. The strategy of each player, originally, was to incapacitate as many opponents as possible with his lacrosse stick and then try to score a goal.

Intertribal games of lacrosse were played for many different reasons. Disputes between tribes were often settled on the outcome of a single match, and the sport was used as a means of training young warriors for battle.

11

Originated long ago by North American Indian tribes, baggataway was the forerunner of modern lacrosse.

The games themselves could vary from contest to contest. Some were highly structured, with only five to six players to a side, and boundaries clearly defined. Others could involve nearly a thousand players, with tribal villages serving as field boundaries and play lasting for days. Injuries and even deaths were not uncommon during these mass contests. Not surprisingly, the word "baggataway" literally means "the little brother of war."

Lacrosse as we know it today began to be played around 1840, in eastern Canada, near Quebec and Montreal. So popular was the sport that, in 1867, the Canadian Parliament declared it Canada's national game. Today, lacrosse is played on an organized basis in England, Canada, Australia, Wales, Scotland, France, Belgium, Japan, Italy, Czechoslovakia, and the United States.

LACROSSE TODAY

Many modern lacrosse purists argue that lacrosse is "the oldest and fastest sport on two feet." Whether or not their claim is true, one thing is certain: Lacrosse as it's played nowadays is good, clean, hard, and skill-intensive *fun*.

In the U.S. today, lacrosse is played and enjoyed by men and women, boys and girls, young and not so young, from coast to coast. The experienced lacrosse player can play the sport long after high school and college via club leagues, summer leagues, and even organized indoor competition, while the young player, who, in most cases, develops his skills with the aid of a friendly wall, can participate in youth lacrosse leagues, which, in the past 15 years, have cropped up in every region of the country.

In between these youth and adult levels are highly organized and keenly competitive interscholastic and intercollegiate lacrosse leagues. Over the past 30 years, these have spread throughout the country, and the advent of the National Collegiate Athletic Association (NCAA) Lacrosse Championships, in 1971, have further assisted the growth of the sport at this level.

What, exactly, is lacrosse's big appeal?

Lacrosse, as it is played today, is unique to American athletics, yet it combines many of the best elements of other popular sports. For example, the physical demands of lacrosse are remarkably similar to those required for football, while its individual and defensive team concepts somewhat parallel those of basketball. The free-flowing nature of the game, from offense to defense, over the vast expanse of a large field (allowing spectators to enjoy all of the sport's subtleties), closely resembles soccer. And the speed of ball movement and the ability of teams to attack from, and defend the area behind the goal, echoes the play in hockey.

To me, lacrosse meshes the most appealing aspects of all these sports into

Modern lacrosse blends many of the best aspects of football, basketball, soccer, and hockey into a unique and fascinating game.

a novel and vastly intriguing game. The emphasis on speed, quickness, anticipation, and transition makes for a great spectator sport, and the fact that every player handles the ball and must have a basic understanding of both offensive *and* defensive skills adds to the game's complexity. As we'll see, lacrosse puts a heavy emphasis on *team* play and coordination. Yet, within that framework is plenty of room for individual initiative and creative expression.

As just mentioned, the growth of lacrosse, particularly after World War II, has been steady and far-reaching. In the past decade, the percentage of American secondary schools that offer lacrosse has grown from 10 to 15 percent, with over 700 high schools and prep schools participating throughout the country. At the intercollegiate level, participation has grown close to 25 percent, to almost 300 colleges and universities competing in different divisions. Combine that growth with the steady rise of club and youth leagues and you can say that lacrosse is one of this country's boom sports.

If there's a problem with lacrosse today, it's that it's growing far faster than its trained enthusiasts can teach it. If you're one of the many people whose zeal for lacrosse—as a player, coach, or fan—is great, but whose experience is limited, take heart. This book is for you. After reviewing the rules of lacrosse and how it's played, we'll learn the fundamental individual offensive and defensive skills so crucial to playing the game well, and then go on to apply those fundamentals to more advanced offensive and defensive team play. For goalies, there's a special chapter on goalkeeping, including a number of drills that, over the years, I have found to be invaluable, and, for coaches concerned about effectively using practice time, I have included a chapter on planning and organizing practices.

This book focuses primarily on the *men's* field game, its rules and playing techniques. Women's lacrosse, equally challenging and exciting, differs in ways too numerous to detail here. Still, you women lacrosse players out there will benefit as much as your male counterparts, I hope, from the material on fundamental stick skills, individual offense and defense, goalkeeping, drills, and practice. For those of you seeking further instruction in women's lacrosse, I recommend checking the resources of your local library and contacting The Lacrosse Foundation, Inc., Baltimore, Maryland (telephone: 301/235-6882).

I love lacrosse, its speed, complexity, and nuance. I hope this book will spread that love to coaches, players, and fans alike. Lacrosse is an old sport, but its growth is relatively recent; it needs our conscious support to ensure its future. More than anything, then, I hope this book will remind everyone, drawn by lacrosse's magic, to give something back to this sport worth loving well.

—David Urick
Geneva, New York

Keys to Diagrams

Below is a listing of key elements in the diagrams that appear throughout this book.

◯ = Offensive player		✐ = Player with ball	
☐ = Defensive player		**G** = Goaltender	
⟶ = Path of ball or other play		**A** = Attackman	
┄┄➤ = Pass or shot		**M** = Midfielder	
D = Defense		**X** = Player	
⌇➤ = Direction of movement of player with the ball			

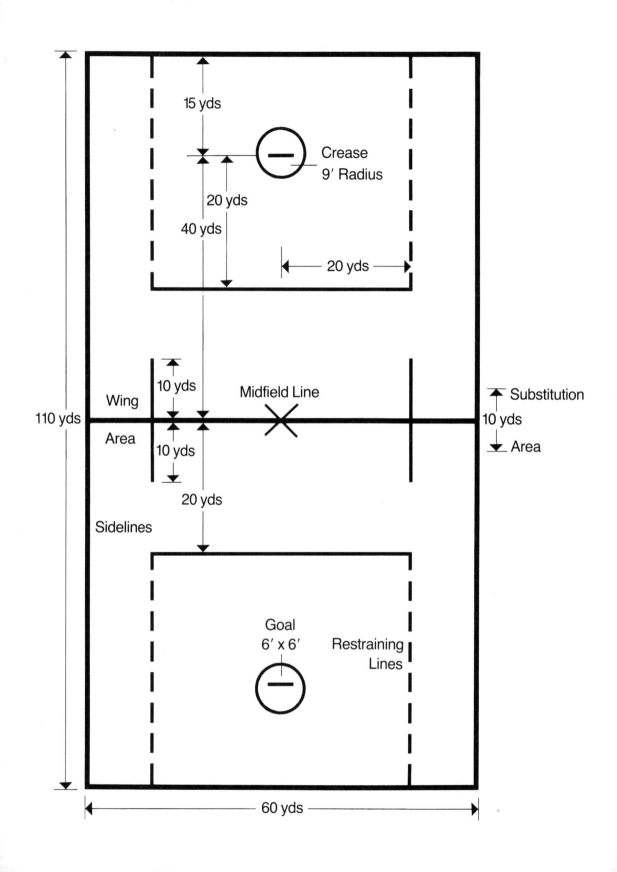

1

The Game

THE FIELD AND PLAYERS

To the novice spectator or beginning player, the rules of lacrosse may, at first, seem a bit confusing. Upon closer examination, however, the game is remarkably easy to appreciate and understand.

The playing area is 110 yards long and 60 yards wide. The goals are 80 yards apart, allowing 15 yards of playing area behind each goal. This large playing area behind each goal is unique to lacrosse and directly affects offensive and defensive strategy. Each goal is six feet square and is surrounded by a circle, nine feet in radius, called the *crease*. The field is divided in half by a center line, and in each half of the field is a rectangular box, 35 yards by 40 yards, referred to as the *goal area*. A point in the center line, equidistant from each sideline, is marked with an "X." Twenty yards on either side of the "X" are *wing lines* 10 yards in length and parallel to the sideline. There is a special substitution area, or *box*, on the sideline marked by two lines that are five yards from the center line.

A team consists of 10 players: one goalkeeper, three defensemen, three midfielders, and three attackmen. Substitutes are essential for all positions, particularly midfielders, as they must continuously range from goal to goal, and can tire quickly. Defensemen and attackmen for the most part restrict their play to half the field. The goalies normally operate in the crease area and around the goal.

PLAYING THE GAME

Collegiate lacrosse games are 60 minutes long (divided into 15 minute quarters), with tie games decided by sudden death play. High school teams play 10 minute quarters with tie contests decided by no more than two three-minute

17

A modern lacrosse field, showing markings and dimensions.

The size of a lacrosse field allows players ample room to showcase their talents.

overtime periods followed by sudden death play in the event of a continued tie. After every goal and at the beginning of each period, the players align for a face-off, a specialized skill described in detail in Chapter Eleven. This method of putting the ball into play is very interesting and unique in that the players are initially restricted to specific areas of the field: The goalie and three players align in the defense-goal area, three players in the attack-goal area, one player in each of the wing areas and the face-off man at the center of the field. The referee places the ball on the ground between the heads of the face-off midfielders' sticks. When the whistle sounds to initiate play, the midfielders are released and compete for ball possession. The players in the respective goal areas must remain in their areas until a player on either team gains possession of the ball or the ball crosses either goal area line.

Play continues after the face-off with each team trying to advance, by running or passing the ball, toward the goal and score. A goal is scored when the entire ball crosses the plane of the 6 ft. by 6 ft. goal. Although most goals result directly from a shot, it is legal to bat or kick the ball at the goal.

At all times, each team must have three players located on the attack half of the field and four players on the defensive side of the field. Defensemen and attackmen are by no means restricted to their respective halves of the field. They may cross the midline at any time, provided the offside rule is satisfied with players from other positions. Normally, the responsibility rests with the midfielders to stay onside in the event a defenseman or attackman crosses the midline.

The vastness of the playing area, combined with the onside restrictions, ensures a fast moving, wide open game with plenty of scoring opportunities. Aggressive play with stick and body checking is permissible within the framework of the rules. Players may enter the game on the fly, as in hockey, or whenever play has been suspended by the officials.

Lacrosse has an additional interesting feature which is unique to team competition. As in other team sports, when the lacrosse ball is thrown, checked, or carried out of bounds, the opposing team is awarded possession. However, in lacrosse, a shot taken at the goal that goes out of bounds is awarded to the team closest to the ball at the exact time it crosses the boundary line. This rule encourages scoring by allowing the offense to maintain control of the ball after a missed shot goes out of bounds.

PENALTIES

The rules and regulations governing the game are explained very clearly in the official NCAA Lacrosse Guide. These rules are enforced during a game by a crew of either two or three officials. Penalties in lacrosse are classified as either *personal* or *technical fouls.*

Personal fouls are more serious and usually carry a one minute suspension of the offending player from the game. At the discretion of the referee, severe abuse of the rules can result in a three minute suspension and possible expulsion from the game. These penalties are rare and usually result from players fighting or from deliberate and excessive stick-slashing. For the most part personal fouls are one minute suspensions served in a sideline area called a penalty box, and consist of the following:

1. *Slashing:* Striking an opponent on any part of his body other than the gloved hand on the stick.

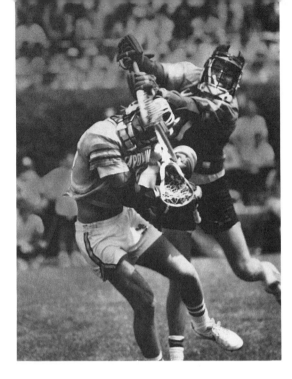

Over-aggressive defenders risk being called for personal fouls. Here, the defender is guilty of slashing. Penalty: one minute.

2. *Tripping:* Obstructing an opponent at, or below the knees with the stick, hands, arms, feet, or legs.

3. *Illegal body checking:* Body checking an opponent from the rear, above the shoulders, below the knees, or when the opponent is not in possession of the ball or within five yards of a loose ball.

Body checking is legal within five yards of a loose ball, but it is illegal to body block an opponent while he is on the ground, as the player in the left background is doing.

A

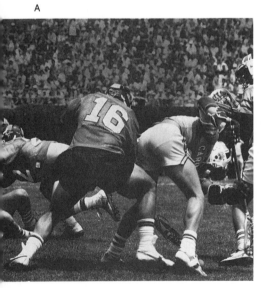

B

Checking an opponent with the area of the shaft handle between the gloved hands is also a one-minute infraction.

4. *Cross-checking:* Checking an opponent with that part of the stick which is between the hands.

5. *Unsportsmanlike conduct:* Any act considered unsportsmanlike by the official.

Technical fouls are less severe and are enforced differently, depending on which team has possession of the ball at the time of the infraction. In a loose ball situation, or if the offending team has the ball, the penalty is simply loss of possession to the opposition. If the fouled team has possession at the time of a technical foul, the penalty is suspension from the game for thirty seconds, served by one member of the offending team.

1. *Offside:* A team with fewer than three players in its attack half of the field or fewer than four players in its defensive half of the field is considered to be offside.

2. *Holding:* Holding an opponent or stick. A player may *hold off* an opponent in possession of the ball or within five yards of a loose ball with either closed, gloved hand on the handle of his stick or with either forearm. However, both hands of the defender must be on the stick. When holding off, a player must only exert pressure equal to that of his opponent.

3. *Pushing:* Pushing an opponent with the stick, from the rear, or when he is not within five yards of the ball is illegal. Pushing an opponent from the front or side is legal if executed with either closed, gloved hand on the handle of the stick, or with either forearm, provided the pusher keeps both hands on his own stick.

4. *Interference:* Interfering in any manner with the free movement of an opponent is illegal except when that opponent has possession of the ball or is within five yards of a loose ball.

5. *Illegal action with the stick:* Throwing the stick, or taking part in the play of the game, but without a stick.

6. *Illegal procedure:* Any violation of substitution rules, delaying the game, or violating any rules relating to the crease area.

7. *Withholding the ball from play:* Lying on a loose ball on the ground or trapping it with a stick for a time longer than necessary to control the ball and pick it up with one continuous motion.

In the event that neither team has possession when a technical foul is committed, the ball is awarded to the fouled team at the spot of the foul. No penalty time is served in this situation.

Lacrosse has a unique slow whistle procedure which is employed any time a defender commits a foul against an attacking player who has possession of the ball in the attack half of the field. The official will drop a signal flag and allow play to continue until the attacking team either loses control of the ball, fails to move toward the goal, or takes a shot. Only one shot is allowed. If a goal is scored in this situation, the technical foul is erased and no penalty time is served. However, a personal foul is still enforced and the penalized team will face off with a man in the penalty box.

A penalized team must keep a player in the penalty box until he is either released by the timekeeper or the opposing team scores a goal. A player can also gain a release if the penalized team gains possession of the ball in its attack-goal area. Serious violations—expulsion fouls and unsportsmanlike conduct fouls—require that the full time always be served.

The novice may find these rules puzzling. However, the pieces generally all fall into place as one watches a game unfold on the large playing field.

EQUIPMENT

The key piece of equipment for any lacrosse player today is his stick. Players should be educated at an early age to care for and take pride in their sticks. By learning to string and restring his stick, the young player not only personalizes it but also gains useful insights into just how it functions. Lacrosse sticks must be between 40 and 72 inches in overall length. Midfielders and attackmen generally prefer sticks close to the minimum length for maneuvering ease, while defensemen usually operate with a stick close to the six-foot maximum for ease in stick checking (more on stick checking later). Lacrosse rules require that the depth of the pocket for all sticks shall not exceed the width of the ball. When examined at eye level, the pocket cannot sag so the entire ball can be seen below the bottom of the sidewall of the stick. There are no restrictions on the length of the goalie stick, nor the depth of the pocket.

Lacrosse has undergone many rule and equipment changes since its inception, but perhaps none has had as much impact on the game as the synthetic or plastic stick. Before the late 1960s, lacrosse sticks were made of handcrafted wood. It was not uncommon for a player to spend hours examining stacks of wooden sticks, seeking the one that felt just right, only to have it crack or break early in the season. Fiberglass could prolong the life of a slightly cracked stick, but jeopardized the stick's balance with the addition of unwanted weight. Moisture in any form, particularly rain, would wreak havoc with the gut sidewalls and throat guards, making accurate throwing and catching extremely difficult. The molded plastic stick heads used today are extremely light, perfectly balanced, and have interchangeable shafts of either wood or aluminum. They have revolutionized both offensive and defensive lacrosse. With these new heads, young developing players can master fundamental passing, scooping, dodging, and shooting skills with either hand. Previously, with wooden stick heads, it was difficult to develop expertise with either hand, particularly for defensemen with longer, heavier sticks. More efficient ball control coupled with increased shooting accuracy with the plastic stick has opened up the game offensively. Additionally, the lightweight shafts and heads have paved the way for a greater variety of defensive checks and have enabled defensemen to become more sophisticated and offense minded in their approach to the game. It is not unusual for some defensemen to carry the ball to the attack-goal area, stay involved in the scoring thrust, and ultimately take a shot.

A protective helmet with a face mask and a pair of padded gloves are required pieces of equipment. Recent rule changes at the college level require all helmets to have a four point rather than a two point hookup for the chin strap. Mouthpieces are also now mandatory, and lacrosse gloves cannot be altered to allow the fingers to leave the protective padding of the glove.

Although not required, arm pads and shoulder pads are advisable gear for all players. Rib pads are also optional, but all offensive players should strongly consider taking advantage of that added protection. In general, protective equipment designed for lacrosse players today is extremely light and not at all restrictive. Thus, there is no legitimate reason for a player not to be adequately protected.

Proper footwear is critical for any athlete and lacrosse is no exception.

Sticks

Here we can see the evolution of the lacrosse stick. The traditional wooden sticks at the top of the picture have given way to sticks with molded plastic heads and removable aluminum or wooden shafts. Pictured from the bottom are: a typical attack-midfield stick, a goalie stick, and a defense stick.

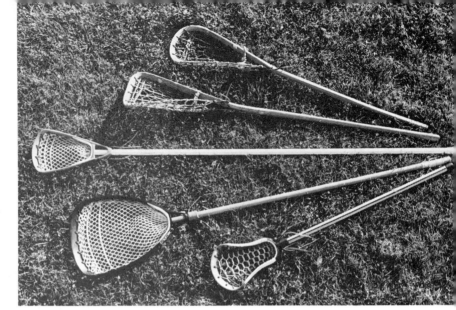

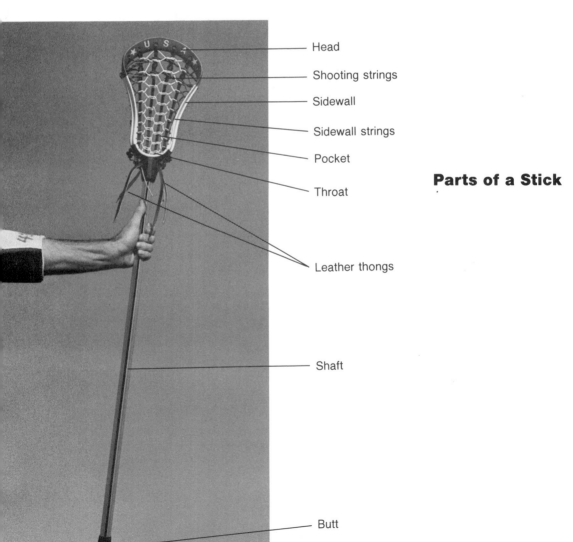

Head

Shooting strings

Sidewall

Sidewall strings

Pocket

Throat

Parts of a Stick

Leather thongs

Shaft

Butt

Other Equipment

Lacrosse equipment has improved tremendously over the years and now provides excellent lightweight protection for the athlete. Shown here, a standard set of equipment that includes: helmet, shoulder pads, arm pads, rib pads, gloves, and shoes.

Cleated shoes designed for football or soccer are fine for most lacrosse field surfaces. However, a reliable pair of sneakers or turf shoes may be necessary when playing on artificial surfaces.

A few extra minutes spent caring for your equipment is time well spent. A good lacrosse player never takes his equipment, particularly his stick, for granted. A little extra care and attention given to your equipment will help prevent untimely malfunctions, and may even give you that extra competitive edge.

POSITIONS

One of the many great attractions of lacrosse is that an athlete can begin the sport at almost any level and, with proper dedication, reach a high level of proficiency. Indeed, many lacrosse All-Americans were first exposed to the game as freshmen in college. There have also been many great lacrosse players who, by today's standards, would have been eliminated from other sports because of their size. Lacrosse players come in all sizes and shapes, but there will always be a place for the "little man" who can complement his fundamental skills with quickness and determination.

Players at each position must master the basic stick skills of catching, throwing, scooping, and dodging. The way lacrosse has evolved today, there is much more interaction and overlapping of the designated field positions. Each position has its own particular skills and requirements.

Goal

A key position for any lacrosse team is the goalie. Not only is he ultimately responsible for preventing the opposition from scoring, but to be effective, he must also lead the defense, direct the clearing patterns, and provide that intangible cohesion that binds a team together. Physically, a goalie must be quick and agile. Running speed is not critical, but excellent hand-eye coordination is a real necessity. The ability to concentrate on the ball at all times and simultaneously anticipate and lead the team defense makes goaltending a very demanding position.

Since the goalie's primary responsibility is to stop the ball any way he legally can, a critical consideration in selecting a goalie is to find a young man willing to stop shots with his body. Many saves in lacrosse are made that way, and shots can travel at speeds approaching 90 miles per hour. Therefore, courage is a prime consideration when selecting a goalie.

Size is not a real advantage for a goalie, nor is it a liability. The key qualities of an outstanding goalie are mental and physical toughness, quickness, alertness, confidence, and good leadership qualities.

The Goalkeeper

The key player on any lacrosse team is the goalie. He must provide strong leadership and play with total concentration.

Defense

Over the years, as attackmen have become more polished in their ability to dodge, feed, and shoot, defensemen have felt increased pressure. It's a pleasure to watch the classic confrontation between an accomplished defender and a great attackman in the open are surrounding the lacrosse goal. Quickness and agility are certainly desirable traits in any good defender. Speed is always a valuable commodity, but the ability to act and react, to judiciously apply pressure, and to recover are the real key ingredients for defensive personnel. Although size aids the defender, the days of big, slow, cumbersome defensemen are over. Indeed, on many college lacrosse teams today, the best all-around athletes can be found on the defensive half of the field—a significant adjustment in personnel selection that has transpired over the past fifteen years. The skills the attackmen display with the molded plastic sticks have dictated a change in selecting and teaching defensemen.

A quick, agile athlete who can play aggressively but under control is what a coach should look for when selecting defensemen. Effective defensemen need not be accomplished stick handlers. Most athletes who begin playing lacrosse at the college level usually play defense simply because their lack of stick work limits their potential as attackmen or midfielders. They can, however, become great defensemen by relying heavily on the competitive instincts and skills they have developed in other sports.

Defensemen

Good defensemen tend to be quick, agile, and aggressive. Most play with sticks nearly six feet long.

The Midfield

Considered by many to be the backbone of any lacrosse team, good midfielders need speed and stamina because the position requires them to cover the entire field and play offense as well as defense. Midfield play places heavy emphasis on hustle and determination. There is no question that midfielders are the key personnel in a part of lacrosse which many consider to be the most exciting, namely, the transition game. Good transition-play midfielders need to be good stick handlers and adept at playing ground balls. It's less important that midfielders be proficient goal scorers. Instead, they should show an instinctive knack for that somewhat vague but very real skill of knowing how to play without the ball.

Regardless of their offensive contribution, all midfielders must be sound defensively. An athlete's ability to shift quickly from offense to defense and vice versa are important considerations when selecting midfielders. Midfielders come in all sizes, but they must show they can get up and down the field effectively and be able to play within a team offensive and defensive structure.

Midfielders

Midfielders (like the one here carrying the ball) are the heart and soul of a lacrosse team. Their trademarks are speed, stamina, and offensive and defensive versatility.

Attackmen

Good attackmen, like the player on the right, provide a team with ball control and scoring punch. The best are always durable and mentally tough.

The Attack

The object of the game is to score goals and that responsibility lies mainly with the attack. Attackmen should demonstrate good stick work with either hand and have quick feet to help maneuver around the goal in heavy traffic. An effective attackman must have good peripheral vision and be able to feed his teammates with precision passes. He must also possess the courage and skill to take the ball to the goal himself in a one-on-one situation. The ability to dodge, feed, screen, and shoot can be packaged into any size athlete. Quickness, alertness, and the ability to withstand physical punishment are all requirements of effective attackmen. The attack must be able to lead the offense by the poise and stability of their example.

All right: Those are the basic rules of lacrosse, and the positions. Now let's look at what every player, no matter what his position, needs to know in order to play lacrosse well: namely, the fundamental stick skills.

2

Fundamental Stick Skills

A player must build a solid foundation of fundamental stick skills before learning an offensive or defensive position. Every player must master the skills needed to catch, throw, cradle, protect the stick, and scoop loose balls. Constant attention to the fundamentals inherent in these basic skills is imperative, even for the more advanced player.

The proven formula for success in lacrosse is to let the ball do the work. The lacrosse ball can move faster than any player and it never seems to get tired. You'll thus enjoy more success and better channel your energy if you learn to handle the stick and the ball the right way and avoid hard-to-break bad habits.

SELECTING A STICK

There are two primary considerations for a beginning player when selecting a stick: 1) the type of pocket the stick has, and 2) the length of its handle. The molded plastic sticks used today offer the player a choice of either a mesh or a traditional strung pocket. The mesh pocket consists of one piece of nylon woven onto the sidewalls of the stick. Most goalkeepers prefer this style pocket, as the wide, diamond-shaped mesh helps to control hard shots and keep rebounds to a minimum. Mesh pockets are also an excellent choice for young beginning players. Constant pocket inspection—adjusting the leather thongs, sidewall strings, and shooting strings—is less necessary with mesh, and it seems easier for the beginning player to master catching and throwing with this type pocket.

As players gain confidence they may wish to try playing with the traditional type pocket. This is a combination of nylon laces woven around four thin leather strips which run the length of the head. The leather thongs are adjusta-

31

Future All-Americans often get their start as ball boys
at collegiate lacrosse games.

Pockets

The traditional woven pocket (left) and the newer mesh-type pocket (right). The choice of which to use is a matter of personal preference.

ble and may need to be replaced from time to time. The traditional strung pocket requires more attention and is widely used by the more experienced players.

The correct pocket for your stick is the one you feel most comfortable with. Both types of pockets are used by players at every level of play. It may help to experiment with both types, as they are fairly easy to interchange, but personal preference is the key.

Handle length is also an important consideration. When learning a new skill, any athlete should be given the best possible chance for success. A novice lacrosse player attempting to learn fundamental skills with a stick that is too long may soon become discouraged and possibly develop bad habits. *The length of the stick should grow with the athlete.* Beginning players 8 to 12 years old should not be too concerned with the 40-inch minimum length required at scholastic and intercollegiate levels, since, eventually, the beginning player will grow tall enough to handle a stick that meets these guidelines. Instead, players in this age group should learn the basic skills with a stick which they can handle comfortably.

At the high school and collegiate levels most attackmen use a stick that is at or near the 40 inch minimum length. Midfielders generally prefer a stick in the 40 to 46 inch range. Defensemen traditionally employ longer sticks that can range from 56 inches to the maximum allowable length of 72 inches.

CARRYING THE STICK

To catch, throw, shoot, and cradle properly, you must first learn to carry a lacrosse stick properly. Many common bad habits in the key skills of passing, catching, and shooting can be traced to poor stick-carrying technique.

The hands should hold the stick firmly, but without squeezing it, about hip width apart. The butt end of the stick should never be exposed. A right-handed player should thus place his left hand, palm down, on the end of the stick and his right hand, palm up, 12 to 14 inches up the handle. It may help a beginning player to learn to grip the stick in the horizontal position; however, one should quickly learn to hold the stick in the vertical position, as that is the way it is most often carried. An excellent habit for beginning players to develop is to try to keep the head of the lacrosse stick in an imaginary box adjacent to the head and just above the shoulder. Learning to pass, catch, and cradle with the stick in this "box" will enhance the development of dodging and shooting skills.

The lacrosse stick may be carried with either one or two hands. Players often use the two-handed carry when they have room to run in the open field. However, in traffic, with defensive pressure being applied, the one-handed carry must be developed to facilitate stick protection.

The Box

Carrying the ball with the head of the stick in an imaginary "box" area near your head and shoulder provides a solid foundation for developing passing, dodging, and shooting skills.

STICK PROTECTION: CRADLING

Working to gain and maintain ball possession is a common goal for all lacrosse teams. All players must learn to protect their sticks when advancing the ball up the field or while attacking the goal area for a scoring opportunity. In order to maintain possession, advance the ball toward the goal, and eventually score, each player must simultaneously protect his stick and cradle the ball in the stick's pocket.

The best method of protecting your stick while carrying the ball in it is to use your body as a shield. Whenever possible, you should keep your upper body between you and your defender, thus forcing him to check across your body to reach your stick. Learning to carry the stick in one hand, in the vertical position, allows the ball handler to use his off arm to further assist in protecting the stick. The off hand should be extended away from the body with the elbow locked and wrist turned inward. Dropping one hand off the stick and extending it away from the body will assist in protecting the lower part of the stick. This is a common technique used by attackmen and midfielders. In addition, you must develop an efficient, effective cradling technique to assist in stick protection and enhance passing and shooting skills.

Cradling is one of the more delicate and arduous skills for a new player to learn, yet its importance cannot be overstated. An effective cradle, controlling the ball within the stick, enables a player to carry the ball at full speed in the open field or to maintain possession in a crowded area. The cradling motion not only assists in controlling and protecting the ball but also stabilizes the ball within the stick, allowing you to master the skills necessary for catching, throwing, dodging, and shooting. These skills cannot be attempted without first learning to cradle effectively.

Cradling is the rhythmical coordinated movement of the arms and wrists whose purpose is to stabilize the ball in the pocket of the stick. The top hand on the stick does most of the work while the bottom hand serves mainly as a guide. It is important to understand that an effective cradle is a compromise between wrist rotation and upper arm movement. As your top arm moves forward, your top wrist rolls in the same direction. The arm is then swung back and the wrist rolled back, creating the centrifugal force that holds the ball up in the pocket and prevents it from rolling or bouncing in the stick. Rotating the top wrist too much or over-swinging the top arm will reduce the effectiveness of the cradling motion. The top wrist and arm must mesh together in rhythmical coordination. All players must learn to cradle and "feel" the ball in the stick. Beginners, however, may initially need to look at the ball when cradling.

The Horizontal Cradle

A   B   C

In the horizontal cradle, the top arm moves forward, and the wrist rolls upward in the same direction (A,B). The arm is then swung back and the wrist rolled back toward the forearm (C), creating the centrifugal force that holds the ball in the pocket. Avoid excessive arm swing and wrist rotation, and, with any cradle, learn to "feel" the ball in your stick so you can focus your attention upfield.

The Horizontal Cradle

A two-handed horizontal cradle is the easiest to learn and most often used in the open field without immediate defensive pressure. The stick is carried in front of the body with the hands hip width apart. This stick position allows you to run freely with effective arm movement and maximum speed. Although this cradle enhances fast movement, it does not protect the stick, nor does it put the stick in position to pass or shoot quickly.

The Vertical Cradle

A more commonly used technique is the two-handed vertical cradle. This type of cradle allows you to maneuver in traffic while protecting your stick and keeping it in the best possible position to dodge, pass, or shoot. The head of the stick is cradled in the "box" area adjacent to the ear and above the shoulder. Again, beginning players can help themselves by establishing the habit of cradling, catching, throwing, dodging, and shooting with the head of the stick in the "box."

The Two-Handed Vertical Cradle

Once again, the top arm and wrist work in perfect coordination. Notice how the player's eyes are focused upfield and the head of the stick remains in the "box" area. The two-handed vertical cradle stabilizes the ball in the pocket, making it especially useful when you are running with the ball.

A

B

 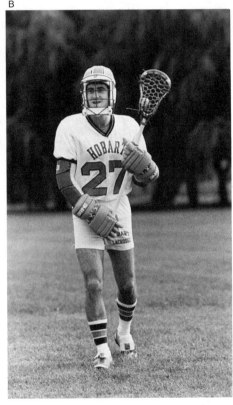

The One-Handed Cradle

The one-handed vertical cradle provides maximum stick protection and is used most frequently by attackmen and midfielders. The bottom hand is released from the stick and extended away from the body to help protect the stick. The top hand is positioned up near the throat of the stick. If you are a right-handed player, keep your right hand below the throat of the stick with your thumb pointed up rather than wrapped around the stick like the rest of the fingers. Adjusting the thumb this way eases wrist and arm rotation and helps to control the head of the stick. The ball is held at about shoulder level so the entire head of the stick is protected by your head and helmet.

Cradling must be mastered before you can effectively learn any of the fundamental stick skills. You must learn to cradle with the stick in either the right or left hand. Smoothness is the key. Developing a feel for the ball is also essential so that you can direct your attention elsewhere, knowing the ball is always ready to be shot or passed.

The One-Handed Vertical Cradle

The cradling motion remains the same as for the two-handed vertical cradle, but now the thumb of the cradling hand points up, the bottom hand is released from the stick, and the ball is held at about shoulder level (A,B). This is the cradle most often used in heavy traffic. In picture C, note how the player with the ball uses his free arm to ward off the defender.

A

B

C

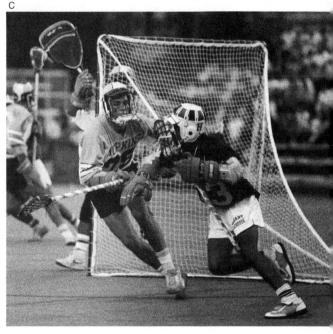

CATCHING THE BALL

Catching a lacrosse ball is a healthy blend of hand-eye coordination, a quick cradling motion, and "soft hands." Offering a good target in the "box" area above the shoulders and adjacent to the ear will assist your teammate in passing you the ball, and help to put your stick in the proper receiving position. The head of the stick should be open to expose the maximum surface area of the pocket. Hold the stick perpendicular to the ground with your hands hip width apart. Your lower hand should always be positioned at the end of the stick.

Following the flight of the pass and "looking" the ball into your stick is very important. Whenever possible, you should catch the ball "near the ear," that is, in the box area. As the ball approaches the pocket of your stick, relax your arms slightly and make a quick cradling motion to secure the ball in the stick and keep it in good position to pass, dodge, or shoot. *Don't extend your arms away from your body.* Instead, keep them in a flexed position, ready to give with the ball as it makes contact with the pocket of the stick.

I enjoy watching great lacrosse teams as they go through their pre-game warmups and stickhandling drills. They inevitably do an expert job of catching and throwing the ball close to the ear. There is obviously a great deal more to the game than this, but it is the major building block of all the fundamentals.

If a pass is not headed directly for the box area near your ear, you must adjust. You could simply extend your arms as much as necessary and rely on the length of your stick to "snag" the pass. The correct technique, however, is to move your ear to the ball. To do this, you obviously have to anticipate and move your feet. Subtly adjusting your body position to insure catching the ball in the box area is important and serves to minimize bobbled catches and turnovers.

A

Receiving a Pass

Receiving a pass requires a soft touch. Be sure to establish a target (A), let your arms and hands "give" a bit as the ball enters the pocket (B,C), and then cradle immediately (D).

Handling the Poor Pass

Unfortunately, not all passes allow you to catch the ball close to your ear. High passes over your head can be effectively handled by sliding your top hand down the shaft of the stick and extending your arms as far as necessary. An extremely high pass may necessitate taking one hand completely off the stick and extending your other arm as high as possible, but you should try to avoid jumping to receive a pass, as controlling the ball while airborne is always difficult.

Balls passed in close to your body can be handled effectively by quickly choking up on the stick. Occasionally, a pass will arrive on the opposite side of your stick and you will not be able to move your body quickly enough to execute a normal catch. When this situation occurs, you must rotate the stick handle and stick head to the opposite side of your body, open the face of the stick, receive the ball, and return the stick back to the original position with a cradling motion.

The Over-the-Shoulder Catch

Quite often, throughout the course of a game, you'll find you must catch a pass while breaking up the field and away from your teammate passing the ball. The best way to handle these wide-receiver type breakaway passes is to catch the ball over your shoulder. If, as the pass receiver, you are looking back over your right shoulder, your stick should be in your right hand. If you are looking over your left shoulder, the stick should be in your left hand. This relationship between stick and head position allows you to run effectively up the field and look back for the ball without twisting your upper body.

B

C

D

A   B

The Over-the-Shoulder Catch

When making an over-the-shoulder catch, "look" the ball into your stick (A), allowing it to nestle in the pocket (B).

When receiving a pass, try to keep your stick up and away from your body. By allowing the shaft of the stick to telescope up and down through the top hand on the shaft, you can effectively reach for the ball. As the ball catches up with you, *look the ball into the stick,* allowing it to nestle in the pocket. This technique is particularly effective for defensemen as they break up the field to receive clearing passes from the goalie.

PASSING THE BALL

The skills and techniques required to pass a lacrosse ball are easy to learn. Mastering the art of passing accurately on the run or under defensive pressure, however, requires constant attention and practice.

Passing a lacrosse ball is similar in motion to throwing a baseball. Since both the left and right hand are involved in the lacrosse pass, you must pay attention to coordinating their motion together.

The Two-Handed Overhand Pass

Accurate passes *originate* in the "box" area (A) and end with a complete follow-through (B). Note, too, how the player transfers his weight from his back to front foot and how he has stepped toward his target for the pass.

A

B

Your top hand on the stick provides direction and accuracy and should be positioned slightly above the shoulder. Your lower hand provides the thrust, or power, and should be placed at the bottom of the stick. Hold your hands high and away from the body.

Weight transfer from the back foot to the front foot is essential to ensure proper throwing motion. Your body should be turned to the side and your feet staggered to aid proper weight transfer.

You are now in good position to make the pass. Start by making a short cradling motion to put the ball in the center of the pocket; at the same time, draw the stick back behind your head. Now follow through with your top hand and extend it just as you would for a baseball throw while pulling the shaft down and back toward the body with your bottom hand. A short step in the direction of the target aids accuracy and ensures proper weight transfer from your back to your front foot.

If you are a beginning player, constant attention to two basic passing fundamentals will help you avoid common pitfalls. First, *the wrist of your upper hand must snap, or break, as you release the ball.* Good wrist snap guarantees proper direction and provides power. A technique I use when instructing beginning players is to have them pass the ball with only the top hand on the stick. This reinforces the idea of wrist snap and helps them avoid the mistake

A

B

Passing With One Hand

Practicing passing with one hand helps teach the importance of snapping the wrist rather than "pushing" the ball. Once again, the player shifts his weight from his back foot to his front foot, and his wrist snaps forward and *down* (A,B).

of pushing the ball. The emphasis on wrist snap is particularly useful when learning how to pass with your opposite, or off, hand.

Second, *you must always complete your pass with a complete follow-through.* Your stick should end up horizontal to the ground and pointing directly at the target. Practicing a complete follow-through will help you avoid throwing high passes, which so often plague beginning players.

The overhand pass, as described above, is the most accurate type of pass in lacrosse and should be mastered before attempting sidearm or underhand type releases. True, sidearm and underhand passes can be thrown with more velocity than overhand passes, and experienced players often attempt them. But they are also considerably less accurate and more difficult to handle, tending to rise as they approach the desired target. My best advice to the beginning player is: *Learn to catch and throw with the stick head near the ear.* Doing so will pay you significant dividends as you learn to dodge, shoot, and feed.

SCOOPING THE BALL

You cannot place too much emphasis on good individual and team ground-ball play. A ground ball in lacrosse is a loose ball, analogous to a rebound in basketball. The team that controls the majority of ground balls in a lacrosse game, or rebounds in a basketball game, is often the more successful team. A scrappy ground-ball player can be as valuable to his team, and can contribute as much to its success, as a great goal scorer.

Unlike basketball, where, quite often, great rebounders also have great size, effective ground-ball players may be any size. The basic ingredients necessary for good ground-ball players are toughness, determination, hustle, and persistence. You can learn a great deal about the mental attitude of a team by observing how they react to a loose ball.

The best way to start learning how to scoop a loose ball is in an open field, without any defensive pressure. As you approach the ball, concentrate on proper stick and body position. Bend at the knees as well as at the waist to help "get down" on the ball as you approach it. Concentrate totally on the ball. If you are scooping right-handed, your right foot should be closest to the ball and your left foot should be back. The head of your stick should be lowered to the ground a few inches behind the ball. In one continuous and fluid motion, scoop under the ball with the head of your stick, gain possession of the ball, and accelerate to an open area.

Proper Body Position for Scooping

Proper scooping technique includes bending at the knees and at the waist, getting the body over the ball, and keeping the pump handle (shaft) low to the ground.

The shaft of the stick in a scooping position is often referred to as the pump handle. The pump handle is controlled by the left hand for a right-handed scooper. The handle should be at the side of the body to avoid jabbing yourself with its butt end, and pumping or lowering the handle down by extending the left arm ensures a smooth scoop *through* the ball. Stabbing at the ball with the pump handle too high often results in a miss, as does flipping the ball up instead of scooping under and through it.

Once the ball is secure in your stick, immediately cradle the ball to your opposite ear and gradually straighten your body. By keeping the stick in tight to your body, you provide maximum ball protection. Now lift your head and focus your eyes upfield to locate teammates as well as any potential defenders.

The key to going after a ground ball, particularly in heavy traffic, is concentration. *Always go directly at the ball;* don't sneak up or round off your approach. Keep both hands on the stick; one-handed scoops are not only difficult to execute, they also make protecting the stick after securing the ground ball nearly impossible.

Alertness, anticipation, and communication are the key ingredients to scooping a loose ball under defensive pressure. Call "Ball!" to signal your

A

B

Scooping

When scooping, stay low and scoop through the ball (A,B). Then cradle the stick in tight to your body (C), and straighten your body gradually (D).

teammates that you will attempt to make the scoop. Try to make the "Ball" call early enough to allow your teammates to react properly. They may elect to move to an open area to receive a pass, or if they are within five yards of the ball, they may elect to body block or shield an opponent from contesting the loose ball. To avoid a technical foul for interference, call "Release!" or "Drop off!" as soon as you have secured possession to signal your teammates that they should immediately stop body contact.

Whenever scooping, you should try to use your body to keep defenders away from the ball. By keeping your body between the ball and your opponent, you increase your chances for a successful scoop, and your body is in good position to protect the stick as you accelerate to an open area. After you scoop a loose ball, it's very important to anticipate where the immediate defensive pressure will come from. If the pressure is from directly behind, quickly bring your stick close to your body and accelerate away in a large arcing path to avoid being checked. Do not make the error, after securing the ball, of slowing down and turning around into the path of a pursuing defender. And watch out for pressure from the side! That can be negated by holding the stick with one hand away from the defender and using your free arm to protect the stick.

C

D

Scooping a Loose Ball Under Defensive Pressure

Scooping a loose ball under defensive pressure requires effective communication. Here, the man on the right shouts "Ball," signaling that he will attempt the scoop. His teammate, hearing the call, moves in to body-check the opponent (A,B). The body check takes the opponent out of the play, opening the way for a clean scoop (C,D).

A

B

C

D

Shielding

Whenever possible, use your body to shield an opponent from a loose ball (A). Redirecting the ball to an open area with the head of your stick (B,C) often makes it easier to scoop.

A

B

C

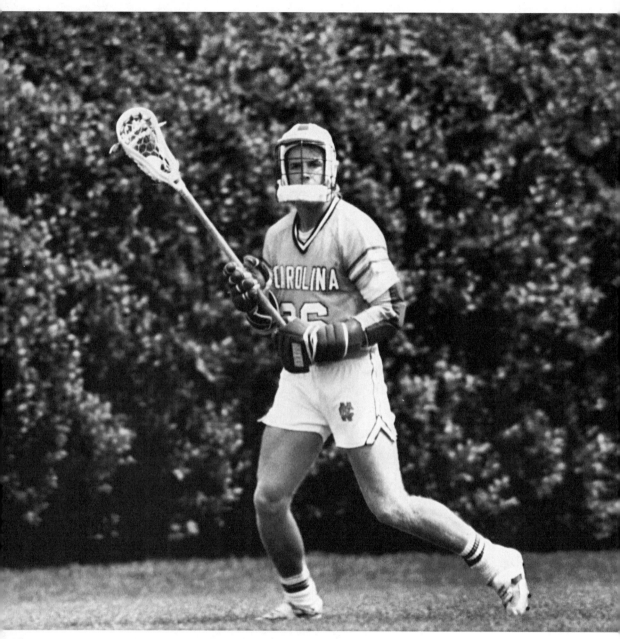

When executing any of the fundamental stick skills, concentration is key.

Half the battle in successfully scooping a loose ball in heavy traffic is *first moving the ball into an open area.* Redirecting the loose ball with the head of your stick or using your feet to kick it to a less congested area are useful techniques which can help you make a successful scoop.

As a lacrosse player, you should take pride in your ability to scoop ground balls. The key points to remember are: 1) communicate, 2) anticipate, 3) stay low, 4) scoop through the ball and accelerate, 5) protect the stick, and 6) keep your head and eyes up after gaining possession.

SUMMARY

A stick, a ball, a wall, and the willingness to practice are all that you need to learn the basic fundamental stick skills. No matter what your level of ability, you must constantly work on these skills. As soon as you are comfortable performing these basic stick skills with your preferred hand, you should immediately start developing your off hand. It's also extremely important to be able to execute *all* the fundamental stick skills—cradling, passing, catching, and scooping—while running at, or near, top speed. Beginning players often remain too stationary when practicing the basic stick skills. Moving your feet while executing these fundamentals is perhaps the most critical key to success.

3

Individual Offense

With a solid understanding of the fundamental stick skills, you're now ready to develop an individual offensive style. The individual offensive skills can be divided into two categories: those used for play with the ball and those used for play without it. Dodging, shooting, and feeding are techniques employed while playing with the ball. Setting picks, cutting off picks, receiving a feed, and screening are the techniques used while playing without the ball.

PLAYING WITH THE BALL: DODGING

No matter what position you play, you should learn to execute the basic dodges. Within the team concept of lacrosse, there is plenty of freedom for individual offensive initiative. Dodging can be a split-second reaction to a defender's action, or a spontaneous offensive move designed to put pressure on the defense and make something happen. Constant attention to proper stick and body position is crucial when learning and practicing the various dodges.

I find it helpful, for learning and teaching purposes, to separate the dodges into two categories:

1. *North-South dodges:* Those executed while moving *at* the defender.
2. *East-West dodges:* Those executed while moving *with,* or hip-to-hip with the defender.

We'll examine the dodges from a right-handed perspective. Left-handed players need only reverse the hand directions to apply the technique to their game.

51

Taking it to the goal sometimes requires improvisation,
as this airborne scoring move demonstrates.

North-South Dodges:
The Face Dodge

The face dodge is an excellent maneuver in the open field as well as in heavy traffic. As the name implies, the face dodge involves bringing the stick in front of your face while moving it from one side of the head to the other. It is most effective when your defender is either slapping down at your stick or rushing at you. Even if he's doing neither of these things, it's often possible to bait your defender into a position that makes him vulnerable to a face dodge. How? By giving the defender the impression, with body position and stick movement, that you are about to pass or shoot. To do this, simply slide your top hand down the shaft, simultaneously pull your stick back and look up field. As often as not, this technique causes the defender to raise his own stick, setting him up for the face dodge.

If you're a right-hander, you execute the face dodge by planting your right foot, sidestepping with your left foot, and simultaneously bringing your stick

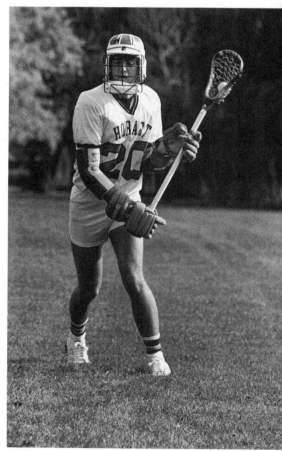

The Face Dodge

Here, the face dodge is performed from left to right. The player starts by planting his left foot (A), then swings his stick head from the box area near his left ear to the box area near his right (B). Once past his defender, he swings the stick in a cradling motion in front of him (C), then returns the stick head to his left (D). Note how the player keeps his head up and his eyes looking downfield.

A

from the "box" area off your right ear across your face to the "box" area off your left ear. Be warned, though: This dodge is vulnerable to a poke check and therefore must be completed quickly. Be sure to keep both hands on the stick throughout the dodge, and, after you have passed the defender, bring the stick back to its original position in the box area by your right ear.

Protecting the stick is obviously very important while executing any dodge. While performing the face dodge, you must remember *to keep your head and eyes up.* Keeping your head up not only provides protection for the stick, but also allows you to focus your eyes upfield for a possible shot or pass. Dipping your right shoulder slightly will help round off your upper body to further assist in protecting the stick.

The face dodge can also be executed with a crossover step. A right-hander will push off his left foot and cross over with his right foot as the stick is brought across the face. Left-handers simply execute the same moves but with the opposite footwork. It is extremely important to keep the head of your stick low enough so that your helmet protects the stick.

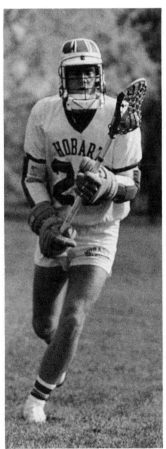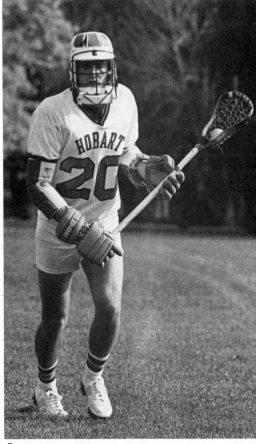

B   C   D

North-South Dodges:
The Roll Dodge

The roll dodge is a North-South maneuver that provides excellent stick protection and can often result in a good scoring opportunity. As an attacker, you can use this dodge as you run at your opponent or when the defender has his stick in a horizontal poking position.

As you approach your defender, try to keep both hands on the stick, maintaining the threat of a pass or a shot. Once you come within checking range of your defender, release your bottom hand from the stick and hold it away from your body for better stick protection. If you are a right-handed dodger, plant your lead foot (left foot) in tight to the defender's body, pivot on the left foot, pushing off the left leg, and step around the defender, always keeping your upper body between the defender and the stick. Sinking your hips in tight to your defender and striving for a 180-degree pivot off the left foot will increase the chances for a successful roll dodge. Your right leg should swing as far around the defender as possible. Rounding off—that is, failing to pivot all the

The Roll Dodge

The right-handed dodger starts the roll dodge by planting his left foot near the defender (A). He then pivots on that foot *away* from the defender (B), putting his back between the

A

B

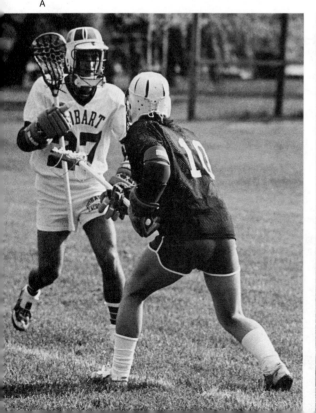

way around your defender—only slows the dodge and allows your defender to recover. To reinforce the idea of making a complete pivot around the defender, practice the roll dodge on a marked straight line.

Protecting your stick during this dodge remains vitally important. As you pivot around your defender, be alert to keep your stick in front of your face and in tight to your body. Problems may arise if you drag your stick behind or carry the stick too high above your head. As you explode out of the dodge (pivot), be prepared to react to your defender. If he attempts to wrap-check your stick from behind (more on wrap checks later), then keep your stick in the same hand throughout the dodge. If the defender drop-steps and attempts to recover, move the stick to your other hand to keep your body between the defender and the stick. *Never change hands on the stick prematurely, only as you are coming out of the dodge.* Keep your head and eyes up and be ready immediately to pass, shoot, or dodge again if necessary.

Footwork is the key to a successful roll dodge and can be perfected only with constant repetition. Lampposts, telephone poles, or trees make excellent defenders to practice against.

defender and the ball. A quick swing of the right foot around the defender (C) and the dodger is free (D).

C

D

East-West Dodges:
The Split Dodge

The split dodge is an ideal move if you're carrying the ball in the open field. Speed and quickness are more important than footwork when executing the split dodge. It is a great offensive weapon for midfielders to use 18 to 20 yards in front of the goal.

In order for this dodge to be effective you must be moving hard enough to force the defender to turn and run with you, hip-to-hip. Once this hip-to-hip relationship is established, you enjoy the same advantage as a football wide receiver in that you determine when and how the move will be made. It is also very difficult for the defender to change direction and recover from this hip-to-hip position.

As the defender moves with you, plant your outside, or stickside, foot and make a quick step back in the opposite direction, gaining ground up the field as you accelerate past your defender. This quick step puts your body in position

The Split Dodge

This is an excellent open-field move. The dodger starts by letting the defender guard him hip-to-hip (A). Then, planting his outside (stickside) foot (B), the dodger makes a quick step

A

B

to accelerate past your defender on a course diagonally opposite the one you were originally travelling. As you plant your outside foot and drive back across the grain, bring your stick quickly across your face. The stick movement is similar to that for a face dodge, except that the split dodge requires you change hands on the stick as you bring it across your face.

Any time you bring the stick across your face, you are vulnerable to a poke check. Therefore, the keys to a successful split dodge are: 1) a quick hand exchange on the stick, 2) driving hard off the outside foot, and 3) accelerating through, and out of, the dodge. As in all dodges, your head and eyes should be up to allow you to anticipate and react to the next situation. If you're a beginner, you can more easily master the split dodge by starting with the stick in your off, or weaker, hand and splitting back to your stronger, or preferred, hand. For example, a natural right-handed player can more easily learn the dodge by driving hard with the stick in his left hand and split-dodging back to a right-handed position.

in the opposite direction (C) and accelerates past his man (D). Note as he dodges how the dodger brings his stick across his face: a risky move requiring that he accelerate quickly after the dodge.

C

D

East-West Dodges:
The Change-of-Direction Dodge

The change-of-direction dodge is similar to the roll dodge and is used mostly by attackmen and midfielders as they attempt to get closer to the goal. This dodge can be used quickly, to try to shake free of a defender, or it can be used more deliberately, to help an attackman get into good position to feed the ball to a teammate.

As the dodger, you should drive hard, forcing the hip-to-hip relationship with your defender, then plant your off-side foot, push off, and roll back in the opposite direction. If you're carrying the stick in your right hand, you should drive hard, plant your left foot, and roll back with your right leg in the opposite direction, using your body to shield the stick. As you change direction, with your back to your defender, you must change hands on the stick, keeping the stick in front of your face at all times. By bringing the off hand to the stick,

The Change-of-Direction Dodge

Here, the dodger drives hard, planting his left foot (A). He then rolls his right leg back, using

A

B

you help prevent dragging, or hanging, the stick out where it can be checked. You may find it necessary to execute as many as three or four changes of direction to get in position for a shot or a feed. When working in front of an opponent's goal, you must step in and gain ground on each change of direction.

East-West Dodges:
The Bull Dodge

As the name implies, the bull dodge places more emphasis on speed and power than on finesse and footwork. By dropping your bottom hand from the stick and using a tight one-handed cradle, you can run through a defender's check. The off arm is extended away from the body to absorb the check. This dodge is particularly useful for attackmen in fast break situations as they come across the front of the goal and are confronted by an aggressive, rushing defenseman.

his body to shield the stick (B). As he changes direction, he also changes hands on the stick (C,D) to avoid a check on it.

C

D

The Bull Dodge

Holding the stick tightly in his outside hand, and using his free arm to absorb the defender's check (A), the dodger literally "bulls" his way past the defender (B,C).

A

East-West Dodges: The Inside-Roll Dodge

The inside roll is a variation of the change-of-direction and roll dodge. It is used most often by attackmen as they drive from behind the goal, above the goal line extended (GLE). Anytime an attackman drives around the goal above the GLE, his defender will often overplay him to the high side, expecting an attempted shot. By anticipating the defender's overplay, the attackman plants his lead foot and rolls back and around his defender with his outside leg. If executed from a point high enough above the GLE (four to five yards), this move will leave the attackman with an excellent scoring opportunity right in front of the goal.

Combination Dodges

Quite often a player will predetermine the dodge he plans to use to elude a defender. Frequently, this advance planning involves performing two dodges in combination. The first dodge is executed in anticipation of a certain defensive reaction; the second dodge is employed to take advantage of the defensive commitment.

A face dodge followed immediately by a roll dodge is referred to as a "circle" dodge. Ideally, the face dodge causes the defender to raise his stick and attempt to check the attacker. The roll dodge follows immediately, forcing the defender to make a second quick adjustment.

The "split and roll" dodge is designed in anticipation of the defender recovering from a split dodge. As soon as the player completes the split dodge,

B

C

he immediatedly executes a roll dodge, forcing the defender to react quickly. This is an excellent move for midfielders and attackmen. The "split and roll" requires precise footwork and may require changing hands on the stick twice. Drilling the "split and roll" in practice presents the coach with an excellent opportunity to critique all the major points of dodging: stick location and protection, footwork, and acceleration.

By simultaneously pushing hard off the left leg and changing hands on the stick, this dodger puts real pressure on his defender. Notice, too, the dodger's head position: up, so that he can see downfield.

Summary

Whether you're a beginning or veteran player, you must constantly practice all the coordinated techniques of the various dodges. It helps to practice the dodges against various token defensive checks to see if you can counter with the appropriate move. Your dodging techniques should become so automatic that you can focus on the field and anticipate your next course of action. As you come out of the dodge, do not relax. Be ready to pass or shoot immediately.

PLAYING WITH THE BALL: SHOOTING

All the individual offensive fundamentals that are stressed by coaches are ultimately designed to achieve success—that is, to score at least one more goal than the other team. Shooting well is the key to winning games. Everything you practice leads to this ultimate goal.

Effective shooting is a marriage between accuracy and velocity. Shots with tremendous velocity that are not "on goal" do little but keep the ball boys on the end line busy. It is equally frustrating to continuously bounce shots off the goalie—usually the result of concentrating on him. Instead, concentrate on the net showing behind the goalie when shooting. Most goals are scored in the upper and lower corners of the net or in the area just off the goalie's hips. Shooting nets or boards suspended in the goal are excellent aids in developing accuracy.

Players generally shoot after one of four situations: 1) coming out of a dodge, 2) from a set position, 3) after receiving a feed while cutting to the goal, or 4) on the run, with the ball on a sweep.

The angle of the intended shot and your distance from the goal are prime considerations when deciding where and how to shoot. As your distance from the goal increases, the velocity of your shot becomes more important. Shooting ranges can be divided into three areas:

1. *Inside shots:* Anywhere from just off the edge of the crease to eight yards out from the goal. This is a high percentage area for shooters. Most shots from this area come off a feed or a dodge from behind (more on these team offensive movements later). Two fakes (at the most) may be helpful when shooting from this range, and accuracy, not velocity, is the key to scoring. Shooting between the goalie's legs can also be successful from this range. Shooters in this area tend to attract a lot of attention in a hurry. Be ready to get hit after shooting from this area. Shooters who find themselves near the

plane of the goal on either side of the cage can increase their angle considerably by extending their stick across the front of the goal.

2. *Medium-range shots:* This prime shooting area lies 8 to 15 yards away from the goal and within an acute angle to it (see diagram). When shooting from this range you must always be aware of the goalie's position in relation to your stick. Again, accuracy, not velocity, is the key. A bounced shot directed back across the goalie's body, or a high shot to his off-stick side, is often effective. It's wise to test a goalie's stopping ability to his off side, that is, to the side of the goal away from his stick. It's quite common for the goalie to lose sight of the shooter's stick and ball as he moves through this area. Shooting for a target is very important. There is a definite distinction between simply throwing the ball at the goal and shooting the ball at a predetermined location.

The Three Prime Shooting Areas and Prime Shooting Angles

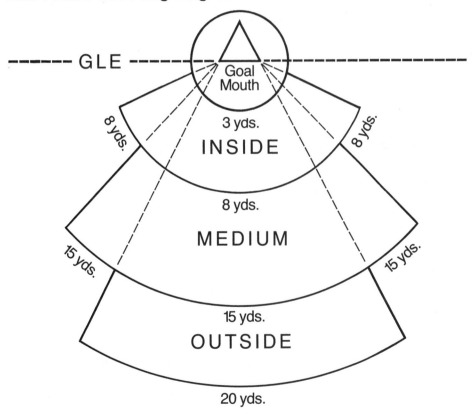

3. *Outside shots*: When shooting from this range (15 to 20 yards), velocity and angle are key considerations. A good angle can be visualized by imagining a set of lines extending from the back lower pipe connection of the goal to the restraining line. Outside shots should be bounced and, ideally, a teammate should be positioned in front of the goal to screen them from the goalie's view. Since velocity is a high priority from this range, you should try to shoot with your strong hand whenever possible and concentrate on getting the shot on goal. Aim for the middle of the goal. Shooting for the corners from this range raises the risk of missing the goal altogether.

Playing Surface

Alert players are always aware of the type of playing surface they are shooting on. A dry artificial surface yields a true bounce, but also enables the shooter, by rolling his wrists over, to put spin on the ball and make it kick. Wet artificial turf will make the ball skip and pick up speed after it bounces. On dry grassy fields, the ball may bounce slowly; however, a hard uneven crease can cause the ball to dance and make life miserable for the goalie. Before the start of a game, test the surface by taking a number of bounce shots on goal, and as the game progresses, be aware of possible changes in the surface of the crease area. In general, *take advantage of the conditions presented to you.* The result will be a higher percentage of scores—and wins—for you and your team.

Shooting Techniques

As a shooter, you should always strive for a positive correlation between shot velocity and shot accuracy. Just as in passing, the *overhand shot* is the most accurate. As you drop the head of your stick to the sidearm and underhand positions, you'll discover that velocity increases, but accuracy decreases.

The Overhand Shot

Properly performed, the overhand shot is extremely accurate and does not tip the goalie as to where you are going to shoot. You should think of the overhand shot as an extension of the overhand pass. Start with the head of your stick in the "box" area above your shoulder and adjacent to your ear, and your hands a foot apart on the stick shaft. As you transfer your body weight from back foot to front foot, push your top hand through with a snap of the wrist and pull your bottom hand down hard on the butt end of the handle. Squaring your shoulders to the goal and transfering body weight from back to front foot will ensure a

A   B   C

The Overhand Shot

The shot begins with the weight on your back foot, the stick in the box area near your ear, and your hands 12 inches apart (A). Now shift your weight to the front foot, push your top hand forward hard, snapping the wrist, and pull down hard on the butt end of the stick (B). At the follow-through, your top arm should be completely extended and your weight almost entirely on the front foot (C).

complete follow-through and aid accuracy. Almost all shots attempted from the inside range (three to five yards from the goal) should be overhand. Occasionally, when shooting from the side of the goal, you'll need to drop the head of your stick to improve your shooting angle. If you're a young player, it's important for you to begin with the overhand shot and to stay with it.

The Sidearm Shot

Overhand shots are preferable when shooting from medium range, but occasionally a sidearm release makes sense. The sidearm shot provides more velocity than the overhand shot, but it's less accurate and more difficult to execute on

The Sidearm Shot

The sidearm shot can generate great velocity. The shooter drops the head of his stick to waist level, sliding the top hand down, bringing the hands closer together (A). He then pushes the stick forward with his top hand, pulls hard with his bottom hand and steps toward the target (B,C). The handle travels parallel to the ground and the shot is quick and succinct (D).

A

the run. To shoot sidearm, drop the head of your stick to waist level and slide your top hand down, bringing your hands closer together. Push the stick through with the top hand and pull hard with the bottom hand. For power, transfer your weight from the back to the front foot as you execute the shot. The path of the head of the stick should be below the shoulder, and the handle should travel parallel to the ground. Note, too, that the entire shot, from start to finish, is quick and short, not broad and sweeping.

You must constantly practice the sidearm shot to ensure an acceptable percentage of shots on goal. Midfielders firing from the outside range (15 to 20 yards) often rely on the sidearm shot. Dropping the head of the stick to the side can help you elude a check and may cause the goalie to lose sight of the ball.

The Backhand Shot

The backhand shot can both increase shooting angle and pull the goalie out of position. The shooter starts by moving to one side of the goalmouth (A), then raises his stick behind him (B), and with a quick, hard flicking motion, shoots over his shoulder (C). The backhand shot is difficult to master, and in games should be performed only be experienced shooters.

A

B

B   C   D

The Backhand Shot

The backhand shot is used for the purpose of surprise or to increase the shooting angle. *It is not a high-percentage shot and should be attempted only by experienced players.* Occasionally, you'll find yourself on the edge of the crease, close to the GLE, with your stick to the outside or toward the sideline. By bringing the stick back over your shoulder, you can shoot from a wider angle on goal and successfully elude defensive checks. If you're on the right side of the goal, near the GLE, with the stick in your right hand, you can increase your shooting angle by swinging your stick around behind your back and shooting over your left shoulder. Keep in mind, though, that most coaches would rather their shooters, when faced with such poor angle shots, roll back across the plane of the goal, change hands on the stick, and take an overhand shot, facing the goal at a good angle. Backhand shots tend to bring both the crowd and coaches to their feet, but for different reasons.

C

Shooting success requires a combination of velocity and accuracy. There are no shortcuts to becoming a proficient shooter. Practice is the key.

Summary

Shooting is a skill that can be developed only by hours of individual practice. Offensive players who rely totally on the time provided within team practices to develop shooting skills will never approach their full potential. A goal with a shooting board or net and a few balls provide the ideal condition for developing shooting proficiency. A stick, a ball, and a wall can work just as well.

You can best spend your practice time 1) shooting on the run, 2) shooting after receiving a feed, 3) shooting after scooping a ground ball, and 4) shooting while coming out of a dodge. Shoot for precise spots on goal and be sure to practice with either hand. Also, avoid merely throwing the ball at the goal. Feinting with the head and stick can further increase shooting proficiency. There are no shortcuts to becoming a good shooter. You must practice the types of shots you will most likely use in a game.

There are various types of postgame statistics that lacrosse coaches examine when evaluating team performance. A healthy percentage (40 percent) of assisted goals (that is, goals scored after a pass from a teammate) is a good indication of team offensive execution. Assisted goals put pressure on your opponent's defense and its goalie. Assists are also a sign that your players are moving well off the ball and looking unselfishly to help create scoring opportunities. Well-balanced teams are comprised of players who can dodge as well as feed.

Most feeds come from the attack as they work behind, or to the sides of, the goal. It is best for an attackman with the ball to be a threat to dodge as well as feed. A pure feeder runs the risk of being heavily overplayed and forced to pass from great distances. A pure dodger will often face defenses that are quick to back up or double team. Off-the-ball movement can come to a screeching halt when a player monopolizes the ball, looking to go one-on-one all the time.

The Prime Feeding Areas

Attackmen will often receive the ball or initiate dodges at the point. However, they should maneuver to feed from the shaded areas.

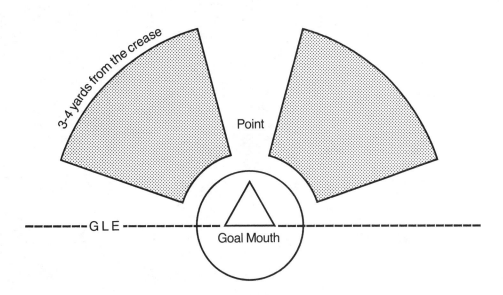

It's extremely important that feeders work near the goal, keep their head and eyes up, and anticipate when a teammate will pop open in front of the goal. The challenge for a feeder is to free his stick enough from defensive pressure to allow him to make an accurate pass to the stick-side "box" area of his open teammate.

There are a few basic techniques that you can use to help free your stick for a feed. Driving hard, planting your offside foot, rolling back, and changing hands on the stick will provide you with time and space. Since, during the roll, you will momentarily have your back to your teammate, timing is important when attempting to feed while coming out of this change-of-direction dodge.

Head and stick fakes that draw the defender's stick up may allow you to drop the head of your stick and feed sidearm. You can also look your defender off, (that is, focus your attention away from the intended receiver), then at the last instant plant your inside foot and step back to pass. The threat of a dodge from behind helps to bring the defender's stick down and allows you to complete an accurate overhand pass.

Proper touch is important when executing a feed. Short, quick passes or feeds to wide open teammates should not be made too hard. A spot feed into heavy traffic, however, must get there quickly. Location is the key. Always concentrate on feeding the ball to the "box"—that imaginary space above the receiver's shoulder.

Feeding

Effective feeders must successfully maneuver under heavy defensive pressure near the crease. Here, the feeder fakes an overhand feed (A), drawing the defender's stick up. He then drops his stick parallel to the ground (B), and gets off a successful sidearm feed (C).

A

PLAYING WITHOUT THE BALL: CUTTING

One of the prettiest scoring plays to observe unfolding is a well executed feed to a cutting midfielder. The cutting game puts pressure on your opponent's team defense, particularly the goalie. Offensive players who execute well-timed cuts toward the goal help to break down immediate backup help for the defender guarding the ball. That helps to create useful dodging situations. Scoring opportunities that originate with passes from behind the goal to cutting midfielders force the goalie to turn and make split-second reactions to point-blank shots.

Timing is the key element of a successful cutting game. The area in front of the goal can become heavily congested if three of your offensive players elect to cut at the same time. A cutter must also coordinate his move to the goal to coincide with the proximity of the feeder to the goal. It's a waste of time and energy to make a great cut if the feeder has his back to you, or is too far behind the goal to make an effective pass.

A simple give-and-go will often catch the defense on its heels and result in a good scoring opportunity. Head and eye fakes used with a change-of-pace move can also help free up a cutter. Driving hard, right at your defender, and then executing a quick stutter step to one side or the other is another useful

B

C

cutting technique. Changing hands on the stick as you cut is a good way to influence a defender into overplaying you to one side. A good cutter must be clever enough to gain a step or two and then accelerate to the ball.

As you begin to break open when cutting, your stick should be low in the "box" area on the side to which you are breaking. Give the feeder a target but always be ready for a poor pass. An open stick in front of the goal will attract immediate attention. Therefore, when cutting *you must concentrate and discipline yourself not to reach for the feed.* Receive the ball back by your ear, cradle once, take a good look at the goal, and shoot without bringing the stick back behind your shoulder. A "quick stick"—that is, a catch and shot in one motion—may be necessary in heavy traffic or if you are quickly running out of good shooting angle. Never bat at the ball. Most cutters have a tendency to rush their shots when in tight to the goal. You almost always have more time than you think. Be prepared to stop and roll back across the front of the goal if you receive the feed too late and do not have a good shooting angle.

Just as a boxer uses numerous jabs throughout a fight, a cutter must deal in constant movement, realizing that eventually he will pop open and score. Avoid clogging the crease area after a cut. Pick and repick quickly with the crease attackman (more on picks in a moment), or move back upfield to balance the offense and set up another cut.

PLAYING WITHOUT THE BALL: SETTING AND USING PICKS

Most offensive players do not realize the total value of a pick and all its options until after they are through competing. An offensive player can really increase his effectiveness and create additional scoring opportunities by learning to set and use a pick well.

To set a pick you must be stationary with a firm wide base. Keep your stick in tight to your body in the vertical position. If the cutter is executing his role properly, he will run his defender into you, freeing himself for a feed. When setting a high post-type pick, that is, a pick 8 to 10 yards in front of the crease, be ready to grow roots temporarily as your cutting teammate runs his defender into you. As your teammate cuts by, turn and cut opposite, or pop out for a feed. Keep your stick ready.

When playing as a cutter, it's important that you brush shoulders with the pick during your cut. A wide cut will allow your defender to squeeze between you and the pick. You can help influence your defender by driving hard to your

Cutting

In this high-post cutting sequence, player #20 on the right cuts off a pick set by his teammate, #21. Player #21 stands with his back to the goal and player #20 approaches on the run (A). As he nears the pick, #20 steps wide to his right (B), but then cuts left for the possible feed (C). #21 then rolls right (D), also making himself available for a feed. An effective high-post cutter must brush shoulders with his pick.

A

B

C

D

Picking: The Defender Picked Off Clean

In this sequence, neither attackman (in white) has the ball. The attackman on the right starts the pick by running right up to the right shoulder of the defender (dark shirt) on the left (A). This frees the other attackman for a feed from behind the goal (B), and a clean shot (C).

A

B

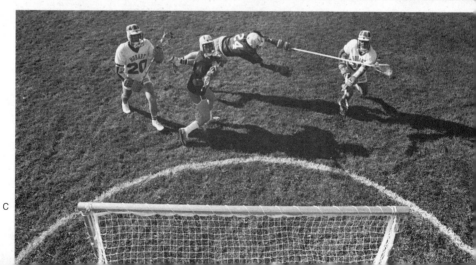

C

Picking: The Defender Goes Below the Pick

Here, the attackman (in white) on the right sets a pick on defender #24 (in black) (A), but this time #24 slides below the pick, threatening to cut off the freed attacker (B). Solution: Instead of moving parallel to the goal mouth, the freed attacker drops back 6 to 8 yards where he is in the clear to receive the feed (C).

A

B

C

stick side as you approach the pick and at the last instant change hands on the stick and blow past the pick on the opposite side. Rolling off the pick is another useful technique for getting open. Always make a complete cut to the edge of the crease and toward one of the goal pipes with your stick to the outside.

When working together with a teammate across the front of the goal, you must try to "read" the situation. Give yourself plenty of room to maneuver and always pick *away from the ball.* If your teammate is moving across the front of the goal to pick for you, be sure to occupy your man with head and stick fakes. If you are on the side of the ball, turn to the outside and move across the front of the goal and pick the man, not an area.

Three things can happen when picking and cutting across the front of the goal. Two of them are good, but you must be able to read the situation.

1. *Your man is picked off clean.* You should receive the feed and have a good scoring opportunity at point blank range.

2. *Your man fights through the pick.* You should now make a full cut toward the ball, then change direction, turn to the *outside,* and move across and repick for your teammate.

3. *Your man elects to go below the pick.* You should be able to sense this and pop out toward the restraining line for a feed, six to eight yards off the crease. If you continue to cut across the front of the goal, your defender will be waiting to meet you at the pass.

PLAYING WITHOUT THE BALL: SCREENING

It's unrealistic for a team to go into a game relying entirely on scoring opportunities from the inside range. As in basketball, it's nearly impossible to get a lay-up each time down the field. Scoring goals from the outside range (15 to 20 yards) can boost your team's confidence and demoralize your opponent. To score consistently from this range, there must be someone positioned in front of the goalie to obstruct his vision.

Screening the goalie is a thankless task but a very important one when playing without the ball. The crease attackman is responsible for most of the screening, but it's not uncommon for midfielders working inside to share the responsibility.

As a screener, you should position yourself about one yard from the crease, facing the shooter, and in direct alignment between the goalie and the head of

Screening

As #6 gets off a bounce shot, his teammate in front of the goal screens the goalie. Note how the screener has already jumped and begun his turn toward the goal for a possible rebound.

the shooter's stick. *Always align yourself with the ball and not with the shooter's body.* Hold your stick in tight to your body. As the ball moves on a wide path across the outside shooting range, you need only take slight adjustment steps on a smaller arc in front of the goal. As the shot approaches, you should jump up, or to either side, then immediately turn with stick ready to pounce on any rebounds or to ride the goalie after a save (more on riding later).

There are a variety of important responsibilities for offensive players without the ball. A player who sets effective screens is every bit as valuable to his team as the feeders and shooters, and a player who can do everything—screen, feed, pick, and shoot—is the most valuable of all.

4

Individual Defense

The expression "Offense sells tickets, defense wins games" may be a little extreme, but the message is quite clear. Solid individual and team defense are common characteristics associated with most championship-caliber teams, regardless of the sport.

Most of the scoring opportunities in lacrosse result from some sort of quick transition from defense to offense. That means that a tough, hard-checking team that is defense-minded all over the field will create many excellent scoring opportunities. A hustling, hard-riding attack sets the tempo for the entire team. Strong midfield defense anchored by alert, close defense can create turnovers and initiate the transition game.

To perform well defensively, you must have a positive mental approach. Take pride in your individual defensive skills and never try to rest or save steps while on defense. If you're a young lacrosse player aspiring to make his high school team, you can attract positive attention to yourself by playing alert individual and team defense. Indeed, given the nature of the game, you will have considerably more opportunities to ride or play individual and team defense than to showcase your offensive ability.

BODY POSITION

Stance

Proper stance and body position are fundamental building blocks for effective one-on-one defense. As a defender, you must maintain a position between your opponent's stick and the midpoint of the goal. A good solid base is critical.

The mark of a good defender is how quickly he can recover after losing a step or two on his man.

The Proper Defensive Stance

Note the bent knees, the straight back, and the position of the feet and stick. The defender's weight is evenly balanced so that he can move quickly in any direction.

Your feet should be at least shoulder width apart, with the foot to the opponent's stick side staggered slightly back. Your knees should be bent, your weight evenly balanced, and your back straight.

As a defender, you should also try to keep your opponent a stick's length away from your body. By concentrating on your opponent's hands, stick, and eyes, you may be able to anticipate the timing of a pass or shot.

Footwork

Whenever you can, playing defense, you should work to maintain a good square position on the offensive player you are guarding. Providing that the attacker is not moving too fast, you can use a "shuffle" technique to stay in the best possible checking position. By taking quick, short lateral steps and keeping your feet spread, you'll be able to stay square to the attacker and react to any change of direction he may make. Never should your feet cross over, or come closer than 8 to 10 inches apart.

As the attacker accelerates, you must abandon the shuffle and establish a hip-to-hip running position. If the offensive player changes direction and attempts to dodge by you, use a drop-step to counter his move. To execute a drop-step, push off your lead foot and step back with your trail leg, then try to reestablish the hip-to-hip running position as quickly as possible. You must be on the alert for multiple feints and dodges from your opponent, and be prepared to execute multiple drop-steps in different directions, as necessary. No matter how good you are as a defender, everyone gets beat from time to time. How quickly you recover is the key to becoming an effective defender. Shuffle with your man as long as possible, run hip-to-hip when necessary, and return to the shuffle when he slows down. Above all, *recover as quickly as possible.*

Stick Position

There are two basic stick positions used when playing one-on-one defense: *cross-handed* and *stick-on-stick.* The cross-handed technique places the defender's stick in the same hand as the attacker he is guarding (right-handed on offense, right-handed on defense). When playing stick-on-stick, the defender carries his stick in the opposite hand of the attacker. Most defensive players keep their stick in one hand all the time, thus playing cross-handed part of the time and stick-on-stick part of the time, as the attacker changes hands on his stick. Some teams will make a conscious effort to play all cross-handed or all stick-on-stick, feeling that this will standardize their teaching and help to better anticipate team defensive slides.

Regardless of the technique you use as a defender, you should always hold your stick at the end and keep its head in front of your man. Avoid the temptation to check an attacker's stick by bringing your stick behind him. Experienced offensive players will often bait their defenders to attempt a check from behind, thereby opening a clear path to the goal.

Your stick should always be kept up, between your offensive man's waist and the top of his jersey number. Avoid allowing the stick to drop between each check that you make, or as you change direction, or when running with your man. Also, be careful not to raise your stick too high near the face mask, increasing the chance of committing a foul.

Stick Position

As the attacker (dark shirt) moves his stick from his left hand to his right hand, the defender's stick position changes from stick-on-stick (A, B) to cross-handed (C).

A

B

C

STICK CHECKS

The best one-on-one defenders combine good footwork and stick position with short, crisp, efficient checks. The stick is not a weapon, and must be kept under control at all times. The most effective stick checks are short (8 to 12 inches) and delivered sharply without any windup or backswing.

The Poke Check

The poke check is to lacrosse what a jab is to boxing. This is a very effective check which can be continuously used without sacrificing good body position. The poke check helps to keep an attacker off balance and can set him up for other checks delivered in combination.

The Poke Check

The defender starts by keeping the attacker a stick's length away (A). As soon as the attacker holds his own stick in both hands, the defender pokes the attacker's lower hand, hoping to dislodge the ball (B). The power for the poke check comes from the lower hand; the upper hand serves mainly as a guide.

A

B

The poke check is a thrusting motion, similar to a pool cue motion. The lower hand provides the power by drawing back slightly and pushing quickly away from the body. The upper hand allows the stick to slide through the glove and directs the check at your opponent's stick or hands. Poke checks can be directed at any part of the handle of an attacker's stick. If the offensive man has two hands on the stick, poke checks to the bottom hand are quite effective. The poke check should also be used any time your man brings the stick across the front of his body to change hands on the stick.

Avoid holding the stick too far to your side. Keep your hands in front of your body to maximize the checking range. A common error when poke checking is to step in with the lead foot. That will leave you off balance and vulnerable to a dodge.

The Slap Check

Like the poke check, the slap check can be used at a comfortable stick's length range, with minimum sacrifice of body position. It consists of a horizontal or downward slapping motion delivered quickly and directed at the bottom hand

The Slap Check

Like the poke check, the slap check is delivered a stick's length away from the attacker (A). A crisp snap of the wrist increases the check's effectiveness (B).

A

B

or handle of the ballcarrier. Most of the power and snap for the slap check is generated by the top hand. Prior to the check, you should avoid any increased stick motion or windup. The head of your stick should move no more than 18 inches to make the check and should be lifted away immediately on contact with the target.

The slap check can be executed from either a cross-handed or a stick-on-stick position. This is a good check to use in combination with pokes. Always be aware that the primary objective of any stick check is to dislodge the ball and gain possession. Keeping your stick under control will keep penalties to a minimum and increase your chances of recovering the ball.

The Wrap Check

The wrap check is a high-risk maneuver for midfielders and attackmen because it is a one-handed check that sacrifices body position and leaves little chance for recovery. Close defensemen with long-handled sticks can wrap-check effectively from a safer distance, and keep two hands on their stick.

If you're wrap-checking as a short-stick defender, you must overplay your man to the stick side. From a stick-on-stick position, your bottom hand drops off the handle and your top hand slides down the stick. Using one hand, you now snap the head of your stick *around* the attacker, aiming at a point just below the head of his stick, in an attempt to dislodge the ball. A short-stick defender playing cross-handed can wrap-check by releasing the top hand from the handle and snapping his stick around the ballcarrier. Avoid being called for a holding penalty by keeping your free hand off the attacker's back.

If you're a cross-handed defenseman with a long-handled stick, you can wrap-check with considerably less risk. Increased checking leverage can be gained by sliding your top hand down the shaft within a few inches of the hand at the end of the stick. By extending your hands away from your body, you can wrap the head of your stick around the attacker and aim it at his stick or hands. Just push away hard with your bottom hand and snap the wrist of your top hand.

You can gain the same advantage from a stick-on-stick position by sliding your hands together and pushing the bottom hand under the forearm of the top hand. The top hand provides the power and the bottom hand provides the snap. Wrap checks have a greater chance of hitting their mark if you can overplay high to the attacker's stick side.

The Wrap Check

To the ballcarrier, the wrap check looks just like the slap check. As the defender's stick head comes forward (A,B), his top hand slides down the shaft and his bottom hand snaps from underneath it, wrapping the stick around the ballcarrier. Here, the defender's check has successfully dislodged the ball (C).

A

Over-the-Head Checks

Over-the-head checks are high-risk, home run type checks that should be attempted only by experienced players. These are all-or-nothing, do-or-die moves that can result in a penalty or an excellent scoring opportunity for the offense. Ballcarriers who carry their sticks too far from the body or with their top hand too far down on the handle are prime targets for an over-the-head check. Recognizing and attempting to over the head only against offensive players who "hang" their sticks will greatly increase your chances of success. You can often set up a successful over-the-head check (one that dislodges the ball) with a few well-timed sharp pokes.

A

The Over-the-Head Check

The defender holds his stick in a horizontal position (A). He then raises his hands high enough to clear the attacker's helmet. Pointing the head of his stick downward, the defender strikes the ballcarrier's stick, dislodging the ball (B,C).

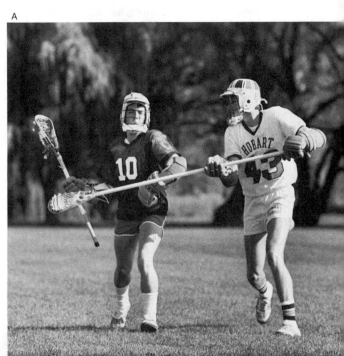

B

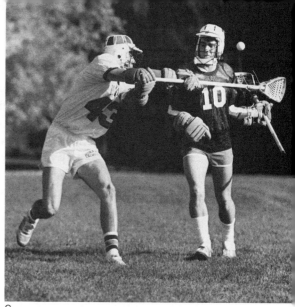

C

The over-the-head check from a cross-handed position is easily visualized when outlined in four stages:

1. Move to a hip-to-hip position with the ballcarrier.
2. Slide your top hand down the handle of the stick, four to six inches from the bottom hand.
3. Raise both hands high enough to clear the attacker's helmet and point the head of your stick down toward the ground.
4. Swing your stick across the front of the attacker, checking the head or throat area of his stick. The ballcarrier will often provide assistance by pulling his stick forward, into the check.

B

C

Midfielders and attackmen performing the over-the-head check must take the upper hand off the stick entirely to take advantage of as much checking surface as possible. A key to the check is surprise. All four phases of the over-the-head check must be executed quickly and simultaneously.

If you're a long-stick defenseman, you can also execute an over-the-head check utilizing the handle of your stick. After sliding hip-to-hip, drop your bottom hand off the stick and slide your top hand up toward the throat. Raise your arm over the attacker's head, and with a snap of the wrist, swing the handle of your stick in front of the attacker, checking his stick.

The Chop Check

The chop check has become more popular as offensive players have learned to successfully counter the over-the-head checks. The key to a successful chop check is to make the attacker think you are trying to check over his head. Most offensive players will counter an over-the-head check by bringing their stick forward, in front of their body. After raising your stick in front of the ballcarrier's face, chop down quickly, just as the attacker brings the head of his stick forward. To the attacker, the chop check appears to be an attempt to go over the head. However, in performing it, you don't need to slide hip-to-hip and sacrifice body position. Note, though: You must take special care to avoid drawing a penalty and not check down too close to the helmet.

A

The Chop Check

In picture A, the ballcarrier thinks that the defender is about to give him an over-the-head check. As soon as the ballcarrier moves his stick in front of himself to counter the move, the defender chops down quickly on it, dislodging the ball (B,C).

BODY CHECKS

Clean, hard body checks in the open field are an aggressive aspect of lacrosse. Anyone in possession of, or within five yards of, a loose ball may be legally body-checked. Body checks most often occur in one of the following situations:

1. As a means of knocking the shooter down as he attempts to shoot.
2. As a means of clearing the crease on a loose ball in front of the goal you are defending.
3. When taking the "man" on a loose ball situation.

It is illegal to body-check above the shoulders, below the knees, or from behind. At no time may body contact be initiated with the helmet. Good judgment and respect for your opponent are the key.

Lacrosse body checking is similar to a stand-up shoulder block in football. Quite often a body check will follow an attempted stick check. As you complete the stick check and move closer to your opponent, slide the stick to the side, keep your head up and to the side, and lower your shoulder, aiming for his jersey number. Attempting to step on his toes will help to keep you from lunging at your opponent.

The best results are obtained by keeping your head up and your feet under you as long as possible. Your arms should stay in tight to the body and both hands must remain on the stick. Avoid rushing at people; be under control. Remember, it's not always necessary to knock someone down. Many times a

B

C

A   B   C

Body Checking

Body-check contact must be made above the knees and below the neck (A). Here, the checker (in white) keeps his body under control and his hands in close to his body (B,C). He must *not* use his helmet to initiate contact.

shielding effect is all that is needed. The primary goal is to gain possession of the ball.

HOLDS

Any time an offensive player penetrates the defense and bears in on the goal, he must be rerouted out to the perimeter. The term "hold" is given to that process of driving shooters out of the prime scoring zones. Close defensemen must be able to reroute attackmen as they dodge from behind or look to feed from in close to the goal. Dodging midfielders who penetrate within 10 yards

A

The Cross-Handed Hold

The cross-handed hold establishes firm control with the forearm (A). A solid, wide foot base helps the defender maintain proper body position (B). With the hold properly established, the defender can move with his opponent (C).

of the goal must also be forced out to the wing area. All defensive players should be able to execute the hold techniques from either the cross-handed or the stick-on-stick position.

The Cross-Handed Hold

The cross-handed hold is executed with the forearm of the upper hand on the stick, which is kept in a horizontal position across the chest of the ballcarrier. As the defender performing the cross-handed hold, you must keep a solid, wide base, with your feet as close to parallel as possible. Your forearm leans on the opponent's upper arm or across his back. You may push the ballcarrier if you can maintain a holding position from the front or side. However, if the hold is on the back (which may occur when an attacker is attempting to back his way toward the goal), only equal pressure may be exerted.

The Stick-on-Stick Hold

The stick-on-stick hold utilizes the heel of the lower hand against the upper arm of the attacker. When performing the stick-on-stick hold, keep your stick in a vertical position to allow efficient checking. In recent years, a variation of the stick-on-stick hold has become quite popular. In it, the defender increases the surface area of the hold by sliding his top hand down the handle and utilizing his forearms or his gloved hands on the side or back of the attacker.

Both types of holds require the defender to get very close to his opponent. This is a potentially vulnerable position, as it allows the attacker an excellent opportunity to maneuver past the defender without much time or space to

B

C

The Stick-on-Stick Hold

The stick-on-stick hold requires that the defender slide his top hand down near his bottom hand. The heel of the lower hand presses against the upper arm of the attacker.

Throughout the hold, the defender maintains a wide base.

His foot position allows him to move with his man while maintaining contact with him.

The key to effective defense? Apply controlled pressure and recover quickly from being faked by your opponent.

recover. Concentrate on keeping a wide base and avoid stepping in toward the ballcarrier with your lead leg. Stepping in with the lead leg will invite a roll dodge that is difficult to counter from this close range.

SUMMARY

An effective one-on-one defender must always rely on good footwork. A variety of stick checks is valuable, but great footwork, combined with a solid poke check, can carry you a long way. It's not necessary to check all the time. Good body position, quick feet, and short, snappy checks are the ticket. Avoid checking in a rhythm. Use a combination of body and stick checks. Poke checks are always good. Since so many stick checks require brisk wrist action to be effective, it's important for lacrosse players at every position, particularly close defensemen, to develop wrist strength for increased checking power.

Accomplished one-on-one defenders take pride in their footwork. To be able to recover quickly requires persistence and agility. Knowledge and execution of the various stick checks is important, but concentrating on improving your agility is essential to good defensive play.

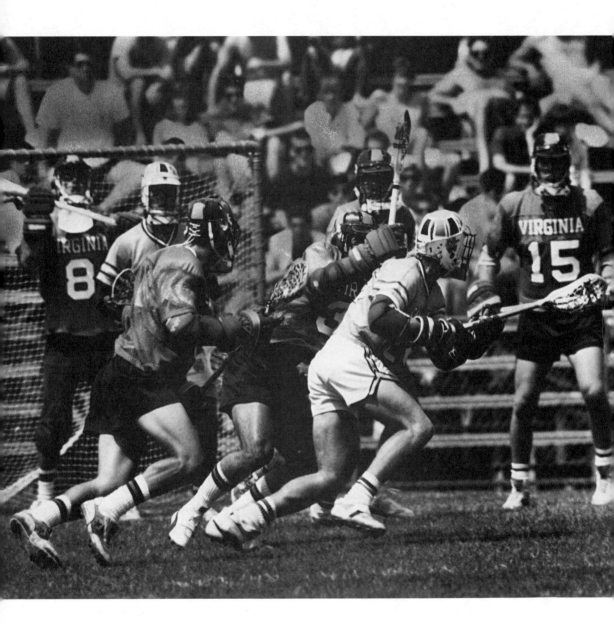

5

Team Offense

Your team's main objective in playing lacrosse is, simply, to score more goals than your opponent. Most scoring opportunities lie in the all-even, or six-on-six offensive situation. To develop your understanding of this phase of lacrosse, you must build on the fundamental base of individual offensive techniques. Your dodging, feeding, cutting, shooting, and a host of other skills must be organized with those of your teammates into a coordinated offensive scheme. There are, obviously, an infinite number of strategies that a team can use in offensive situations. Whichever ones your team uses, they must be understood by the team, lest the players go through the motions like robots, acting with little or no purpose.

Generating good scoring opportunities requires that an offense create a numerical advantage somewhere in the defensive structure. The most basic way for this to occur is for the offensive player with the ball to dodge past his defender, shoot, and score. However, solid defensive teamwork makes this play difficult to execute consistently, so we need to explore more flexible and well rounded offensive strategies. As a player on offense, you should keep in mind that understanding the principles of team defense will help you better execute any offensive tactic.

POWER LACROSSE

Power Lacrosse might be described as trying to create a dodging opportunity for one of the offensive players so that he is left with a one-on-one shooting opportunity against the goalie. The point of attack can be varied; from in front of the goal to behind it, or even from the side, or "wing" area. Of prime

95

Good team offense requires coordinated timing and intelligent off-ball movement.

importance in this style of lacrosse is, quite naturally, sound dodging technique, so the player with the ball can exploit the one-on-one situation against the goalie. It is extremely important that his offensive teammates move to create space for the player with the ball, occupy their defender to eliminate "backups," a term used in lacrosse meaning "double-team" (more on backups in Chapter Seven, "Team Defense"), and be ready to receive the ball, should a backup occur, that is, should an off-ball defender leave his man to assist his teammate guarding the man with the ball.

A dodging situation can be created in a number of offensive configurations. Probably the least subtle formation, involving the three attackmen and three midfielders, is the one-four-one, known in lacrosse as the Isolation Setup. [Note: For identification purposes, the offensive schemes will consist of three digits identifying the offensive personnel located at the top of the formation (midfield), the crease and GLE, and the area behind the goal. (Example: one-four-one, three-one-two, two-two-two)]. As the diagram shows, this one-four-one configuration gives the player with the ball (in this case, midfielder M_1) ample room to set up his dodge and to run past his defender. In the Isolation Setup, the remaining offensive players serve several important functions. M_2 and M_3

Power lacrosse from the 1-4-1 alignment.

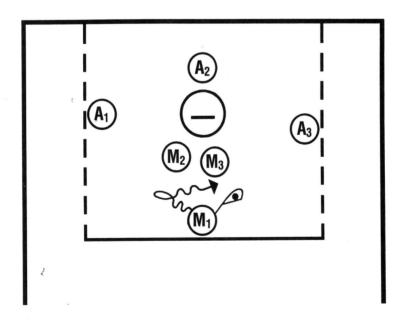

are a threat to receive the ball directly in front of the goal, so their sticks must be in a ready position and their eyes must be on the ball. Another extremely important function for either of them is to act as a screen, should the teammate with the ball take an outside shot. The attackmen (A_1 and A_3), positioned on the wings, to either side of the goal, are in excellent position to receive a pass from M_1 should either of their defenders slide to back up (double-team him). A_2, positioned behind the crease, can stop and put back into play shots that are not on goal (and positioning an attacker to serve this function is important in *any* offensive scheme). In all, the Isolation Setup has flexibility, purpose, and balance.

It's likely that when the defense identifies this Isolation Setup, they will quickly adjust, sending a teammate to support the defender on the ball. The backup man can be any of the other defenders. When a backup occurs, the player with the ball must pass quickly to an adjacent teammate, who in turn can try to identify where the open offensive player is located. Too often the dodging player makes the mistake of attempting to complete the play by himself. He must realize that when he draws a second defender and finds himself double-teamed, he has done his job and must pass the ball to a team-

Power Lacrosse

Power lacrosse relies on a 1-on-1 move to the goal and subsequent reaction to the team defensive adjustment.

mate who, in turn, can identify and exploit the numerical advantage created by the defensive slide. It may take more than one pass to locate the open offensive player, and the ball must be passed quickly.

The one-four-one Isolation Formation can be effective because it is easy for an offense to set up and understand. With it, offenses can also take advantage of some obvious defensive weaknesses. It does have some drawbacks, however. First, it is easy for the defense to identify and adjust to. Second, it leaves the offensive team vulnerable to a fast break situation, since two of their midfielders are down in front of the goal. Other formations allow an offense to flow into dodging situations. The point of all of them, including the one-four-one, is *to create space for the player with the ball.*

Other "Power Lacrosse" Formations: The Three-One-Two

An excellent dodging situation can be created from a three-one-two configuration. In this play, M_2 passes the ball to M_1 and pretends to be setting a pick for M_3. He then quickly changes direction and angles toward the crease area. M_3 simultaneously cuts toward the goal with his stick in a backhanded posi-

The 3-1-2.

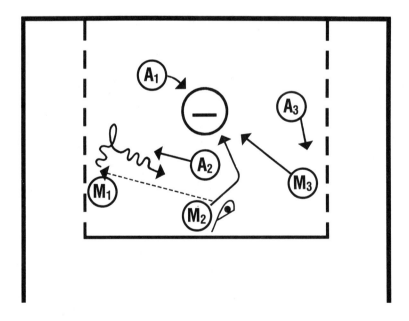

99

tion, ready to receive the ball should his defender not go with him. M_1 now has ample room to set up and execute a dodge, with a good shooting angle afterwards. A_3 moves into position to provide M_1 with an outlet if there is no shot, and A_1 moves to give balance and to back up a missed shot.

Note how this play moves from a three-one-two setup into the previously described one-four-one Isolation. However, it is somewhat disguised, and thus the defense has more difficulty adjusting to it.

The Two-Two-Two

A two-two-two formation can also be utilized to create an isolation play. In this setup, M_2 passes to M_1 and moves to set a pick for A_3. M_1 can now dodge into a good shooting position. A_2 moves up to provide support and A_1 backs up the goal. If a slide occurs, that is, if M_1 finds himself double-teamed, he quickly passes the ball to A_2, who moves it on to A_1 behind the goal. From this position, it's easier to identify the open offensive player. Like the three-one-two, the player movement off the ball also evolves into a one-four-one alignment.

The 2-2-2.

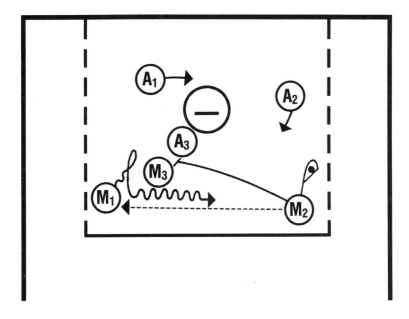

The Three-One-Two With Point of Attack Behind the Goal

By changing the point of attack to behind the goal, an offense can flow into an isolation from a three-one-two formation. In this situation, the ball starts at the midfield and is quickly passed around the perimeter until it reaches A_2, behind the goal. A_3, M_2, and M_3 move to a position beyond the far goalpost, away from A_2. M_2 and M_3 can set picks for A_3 and M_1, but all players must be careful to give A_2 enough room to dodge (shaded area). They must also be ready to move into open areas in the event of a defensive slide. This play can be worked to either side of the goal. As in other offensive patterns, A_1 slides to a position behind the goal to back up any shots wide of the goal.

The 3-1-2 with the point of attack behind the goal.

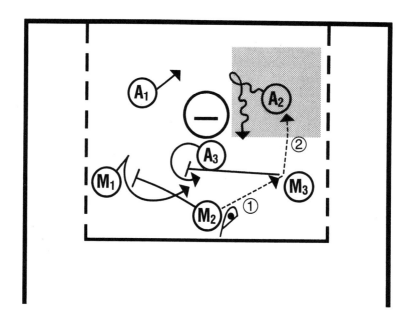

The Two-Three-One With Point of Attack From the Wing

Another dodging situation can be created from a two-three-one set, with the point of attack coming from the wing area. M_3 passes the ball to M_1 and moves toward the goal area. M_1 drives into the area vacated by M_3 and delivers the ball to A_3, who is moving up on the wing. M_3 moves into the area vacated by

The 2-3-1 with the point of attack from the wing.

M_3 passes to M_1.

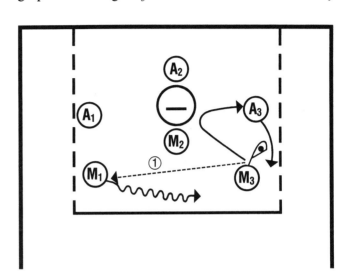

M_1 passes to A_3, who passes to M_3.

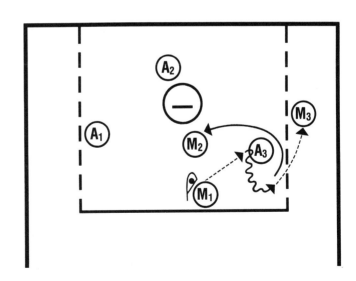

A_3. A_3 passes the ball to M_3 and cuts to the area in front of the goal. The offense has now moved into a one-four-one, with the ball in the wing area. M_3 has a great deal of room to attempt to beat his defender. If a defensive slide occurs, M_3 should be prepared to pass the ball on, especially to A_2 behind the goal.

Power Lacrosse, which relies on dodging one-on-one, can be extremely effective against man-to-man defenses. Zone defenses, which are designed to defend areas rather than individuals, can neutralize Power Lacrosse patterns. As an approach to offense, Power Lacrosse is easy to implement and to understand: The offense tries to create situations where a player can dodge free of his defender and take on the goalie, one-on-one. The point of attack can be changed to suit the team's offensive strength, whether it be on the attack or in the midfield. It's also possible, in Power Lacrosse, to isolate and exploit a weak defensive player.

It's important that the offensive players realize they must make their opponents respect and defend them without the ball, as well as when in possession of it. Their movements must be quick and their sticks must be in a ready position. If their defender slides to, or double-teams the ball, they must move to the open area and call for the ball. *Communication is essential.* When the defense slides another player to the ball, quick ball movement by the offense can locate and take advantage of a numerical superiority somewhere else in the offensive zone. That's the idea behind this style of attack.

THREE-MAN PLAYS

Three-man plays can also generate good shooting situations. These plays are often best generated in the midfield or with the attack, or even some combination of the two. Three-man plays incorporate the offensive skills of cutting, picking, feeding, and shooting, so execution and timing are essential. The plays can be called out with an oral command or they may be executed spontaneously. Midfield and attack units that have experience playing together often-times initiate plays of this nature with some sort of signal or simply by being familiar with each other's movements.

Midfield Plays

One effective way to set up a midfielder for a shot can evolve from a three-one-two configuration, with the center midfielder in possession of the ball. In this setup, M_2 passes the ball to M_1 and moves to set a pick for M_3. M_3 must move

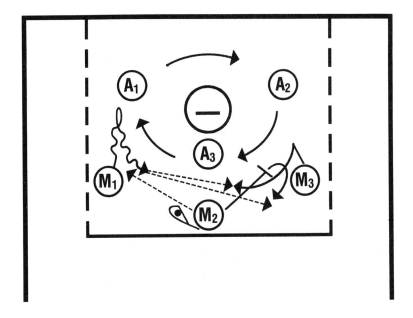

his man toward the goal so that his defender will play him closely. He should have his stick in his right hand. M_2 will set his pick on M_3's defender and not on a space (that is, set the pick on a man, not a spot). M_3 will not cut until the pick is set. He will then switch hands on his stick and accelerate past the pick, trying to get his stick clear to receive the ball. M_1 must move hard with the ball so that the defense respects him as a dodger. If he stands still while attempting to pass off, his defender can easily overplay him and prevent him from making the feed. After the cut, M_2 will curl out to the open area with his stick ready, should M_3 not be open. He is also able to back up a missed pass. If he does receive the ball, he has a great deal of room to dodge past his defender.

One variation of this play can utilize a pick-repick concept which is particularly effective when the defense employs a "switch" of responsibility in defending the cut off the pick. This variation evolves in the same manner as the previous play. However, when M_3 cuts off the pick and feels the defense moving with him, he quickly pivots back and sets a pick for M_2 who, in turn, makes the cut, ready to receive the ball in a shooting position. (Note that, in both plays, A_3 is in a good position to screen the outside shot.)

A variation of the pass-and-pick-away.

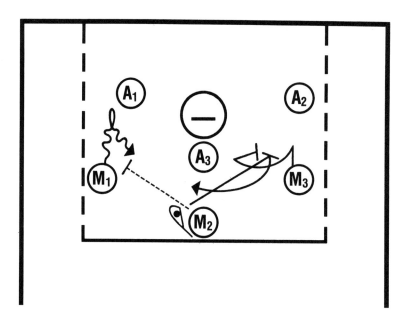

Attack Plays

Three-man plays with the attack also utilize many of these same concepts and can create good scoring opportunities. These plays are especially effective from a dead ball situation on the endline. Again, timing and execution are extremely important. In a basic three-man attack play, A_1 passes to A_2 and cuts toward the front of the goal. A_3 sets a pick on A_1's defender who uses proper cutting technique to free himself. When A_2 receives the ball, he must drive hard to his right and then roll back with his stick to the outside as he moves into the optimum feeding area (shaded area). A_2 must time his move so that he is in position to deliver the ball at the proper moment. After setting the pick, A_3 will cut toward the opposite pipe (the opposite side of the goal mouth) with his stick ready, should both defenders move toward A_1.

A basic three-man attack play.

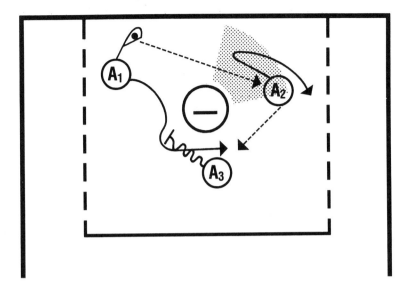

This play can be taken a step further by implementing the aforementioned pick-repick concept. A_1 begins his cut as he did in the previous play. However, as he passes by the pick and feels the defense following him, he pivots with his back to the goal (in this case, over his left shoulder) and sets a pick on A_3's defender, who, in turn, makes the final cut. This pick-repick play can be

Variation #1: a basic three-man attack play using the pick-repick concept.

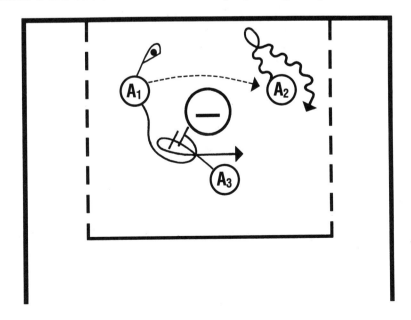

Variation #2: a basic three-man attack play that takes advantage of the defense's reaction to a pick.

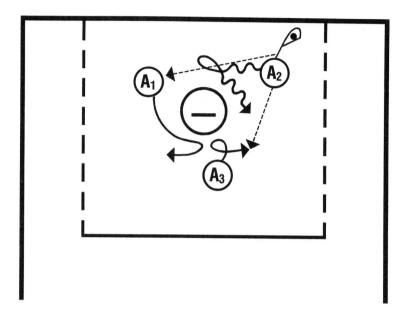

especially effective in the latter part of a game, particularly when the regular cuts have been run a number of times and the defense has gotten used to them.

Another three-man attack play which bears mentioning is set up in the same fashion. In this play, A_1 passes to A_2 and moves toward the pick set by A_3. A_3 moves as he did in the previous play and then makes a hard move toward the other side of the goal. A_1 proceeds until he gets even with the pick and quickly pivots with his stick to the outside. A_3 curls in the opposite direction and A_2 can then feed either player. This play is very effective against defenders who have elected to go below the pick to avoid getting rubbed off their man. (Note that the midfielder clears out of the shooting area, to take his defender out of the play.)

These are merely a few of the many plays that can be utilized in an all-even offensive situation. They can be effective when implemented in a series or sequence. By changing the cutting and picking pattern, the offense forces the opposition defense to honor each and every move, thus creating better opportunities for the offense. It is also important that the offensive players execute the plays with a degree of deception and flexibility. As with most offensive plays, constant repetition in practice, even with no defense, aids in developing the proper timing and execution.

CUTTER OFFENSE

One aspect of lacrosse which is somewhat unusual is the ability to utilize the space *behind* the goal to initiate the offense. Cutter-type offenses, while difficult to implement, are beautiful to watch when executed properly, and usually result in a high percentage shot for the offense. That's because the offense, through the use of picking and cutting, strives to get a player open directly in front of the goal.

Prerequisites for executing this style of offense are sound cutting and picking fundamentals, and at least one, better yet two, attackmen with good stickwork, peripheral vision, and a sense of timing. These attackmen must be able to drive their defenders into the optimum feeding areas, anticipate a teammate getting open, clear their sticks of the defenders' checks, and deliver an accurate feed to the cutter as he breaks free. Good feeders are not necessarily the fastest or biggest players, but should have respectable dodging abilities. The best feeders are generally ambidextrous with their stickwork, have a good understanding of the offense being run, and an uncanny ability to deliver the ball at the proper time.

The offense has 15 yards behind the goal in which to operate. This area can be used to initiate dodges or to feed passes to teammates in front of the goal.

One excellent cutting offense can be derived from a three-one-two configuration, with the ball behind the goal. This formation gives good balance and has a cutting pattern that is simple to follow. In this setup, A_3 acts as a high post that the cutting midfielders can use as a pick. The first rule is that the cutter is always the central midfielder (M_2). He has the option of cutting to either side of the high post, depending on how he is being defended. After the central midfielder makes his cut to either post, he then backs out, facing the ball, to the wing midfield position on that side. Whichever side he backs out, that midfielder fills the middle position and becomes the next cutter. Continuous motion within this cutting system may produce a figure eight type of movement among the midfielders. A_3 can also select his cutting opportunities after the

**Cutter offense
from the 3-1-2.**

The central midfielder, M_2, makes the first cut.

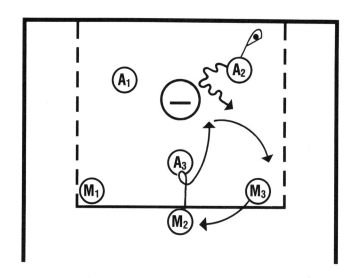

M_3 takes M_2's place and continues the cutting pattern.

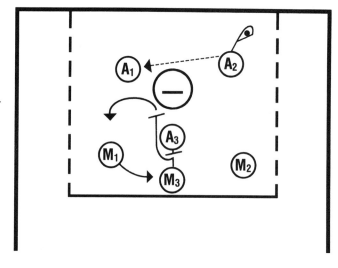

midfielder has cut. A_1 and A_2 can work together behind the goal in any manner, flip passing, exchanging, and picking for each other, all the while watching for a cutting teammate to get free. This is a good cutting pattern to follow because it has structure and continuity. However, if overused, cuts tend to be somewhat predictable, allowing the defense to anticipate and negate their effectiveness.

Good cutting opportunities can be developed from a tandem high post offense. This configuration can give more possibilities for cutting, picking, and repicking. In this sequence, A_2 has the ball behind the goal. M_1 tries to hang his man up on the tandem high post formed by M_2 and A_3, and cuts toward the ball. A_2 passes the ball to A_1, who moves into a feeding position. After M_1

A 2-2-2 tandem high post cutting pattern.

M_1 cuts by the tandem high post.

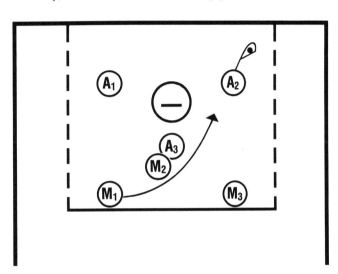

A_2 passes to A_1 who looks to feed A_3 off the repick.

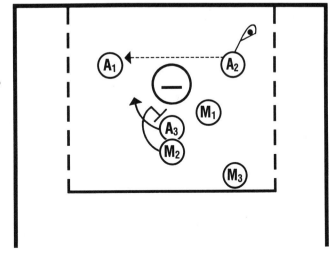

makes his cut, M_2 breaks opposite, toward the other pipe. Once he feels his defender moving with him, he pivots back and sets a repick for A_3. In this play, we have employed a regular pick and cut, as well as a repick. We can take this play further by having A_3 pivot after his cut and move across the goalmouth to set a pick for M_1.

There are, obviously, numerous ways to develop a cutting type offense. Some involve more structure than others. Each takes a good deal of coordination and timing. Many involve a favorite target, much like a quarterback and receiver in football. Something as simple as eye contact between an attackman and a midfielder can set up an effective cutting situation. A cutting offense is exciting to watch and fun to play, as it involves all six offensive players. However, teams must be careful not to overuse this offense, as the defense tends to sag closer to the goal, thus narrowing the passing lanes and cutting areas, making it more difficult to find an open player.

CIRCULATION OFFENSE

A versatile and simple offense to execute can be derived from a two-three-one formation. This circulation offense is versatile, in that it incorporates the concepts of off-ball movement, creating space for the ballcarrier, and for picking and cutting, as well as encouraging individual initiative, with and without the ball. The formation uses a basic principle of two triangles, one with the attack, the other with the midfield. Each attackman may be in any one of the positions of the triangle and tries to maintain this relationship as the offense circulates. The midfielders keep the same relationship within their triangle.

The second concept employed is the use of a "give-go" technique. Whenever a player passes to a teammate, he quickly cuts to the inside of his triangle, with his stick to the inside, looking for a return pass. M_3 passes to A_3 and sharply breaks toward the crease, looking for a return pass. M_1 moves into the area vacated by M_3 and M_2 fills in for M_1. Thus, the triangular circulation.

The ball is now with A_3. If he passes to M_1, he cuts through the crease area with his stick in a backhand position (in this diagram, left-handed). A_2 can then move into the area vacated by A_3, and A_1 replaces him behind the goal. Again, the triangle concept is maintained.

If M_1 now decides to pass the ball to M_2, he cuts through in a ready position. M_2 now has a great deal of space to attempt a dodge into a good shooting position. M_1 can even set a pick for M_3, thus creating another chance for a shot. Each time a player receives a pass, he can dodge into the area from which he received the ball.

Circulation offense: the give-go.

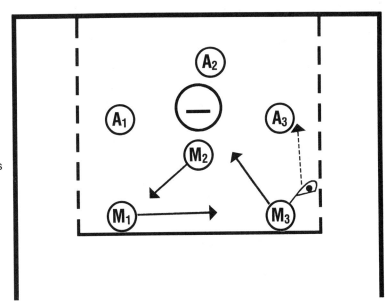

M_3 passes to A_3 and breaks for the crease.

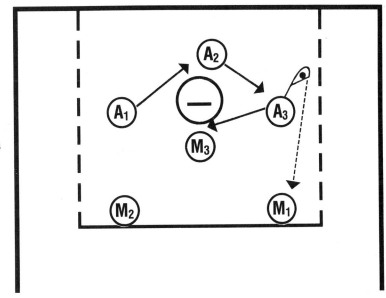

A_3 passes to M_1 and breaks for the crease.

We can see that the formation changes from a two-three-one formation into a one-four-one, and back into a two-three-one, as the triangles rotate. This style of offense does an excellent job of disguising isolation situations. If the players are encouraged to pick for each other in front of the goal, this offense can set up excellent cutting and feeding opportunities. To implement this offense, players need to be proficient with their stick in either hand, as they can find themselves in one of three positions around the goal. They should be encouraged to dodge when the situation presents itself (when there is sufficient space) and to work together to set picks for each other.

ZONE OFFENSE

More and more teams are utilizing zone defenses as part of their defensive package. Some rely on them all the time, while other teams employ them in specialty situations. The rationale for a zone defense is to neutralize the power, or dodging style, of a team's offense. A team should be prepared to face a zone defense, but radical changes in offensive formation and philosophy are impractical, inefficient, and unnecessary. *Coaches should try to incorporate their normal offense in preparation to face a zone,* stressing what will and will not work.

The two-three-one circulation, with a few minor adjustments, can offer an excellent offense against a zone, as it has good balance for perimeter passing, allows a great deal of off-ball movement, and puts players into good shooting positions. By initiating the play with the ball behind the goal, a great deal of pressure can be placed on a zone.

In this adjustment of the two-three-one circulation, A_2 carries the ball hard to his right. A_3 quickly breaks behind and receives the ball. A_1 moves into a shooting position, and M_3 can break into an open area on the far pipe. We now have three players in dangerous shooting positions, directly in front of the goal. A lofted pass to M_1, over the top of the zone, can produce a good shot, as the necessary screen is now in front of the goalie.

Key ingredients in attacking a zone are: 1) quick ball movement, 2) cutters cutting into the crease area, and 3) well-screened outside shooting. This two-three-one circulation offense can utilize these concepts with few changes. Players should be aware that dodging and picking may be ineffective against a zone. Timing, cutting into open areas, and trying to create an overload in the zone work best.

**Offense against a zone:
an adjustment of the
2-3-1 circulation offense.**

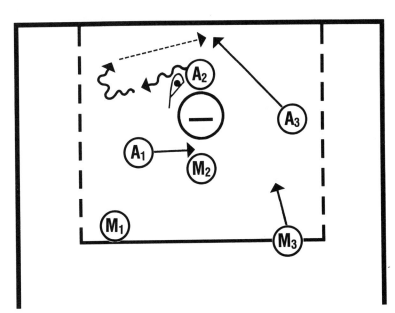

A_2 moves to his right and
passes to A_3.

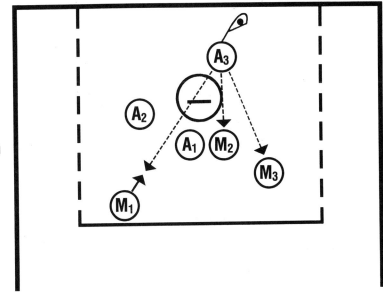

A_3 can pass to M_1, M_2, or
M_3, each of whom has moved
in for a shot on goal.

CLEARING

The primary responsibility of the team defense is to prevent the offense from scoring. Once this immediate goal is achieved, the defense must concentrate on clearing the ball to its offensive goal area. A clear occurs any time a team gains possession in its defensive half of the field and advances the ball into its offensive goal area. Offensive success—that is, goal productivity—is directly related to the ability to successfully clear the ball. Clearing requires the coordinated team effort of the goalie, close defense, midfielders, and attack.

Clearing attempts can be broken down into two categories: *inbounds* and *out-of-bounds*. An inbounds clearing attempt follows either a goalie save or a turnover in the defensive half of the field. An inbounds clear occurs spontaneously within the flow of the game. An out-of-bounds clearing opportunity occurs following a change of possession in the defensive half of the field after an official stoppage of play. This type of clear is less spontaneous than an inbounds clear, and places more emphasis on predetermined player positioning and ball movement.

Both types of clears must be drilled repeatedly. Coaches should constantly stress the critical impact that successful clearing can have on the outcome of a game. Let's examine the two basic types of clears and the fundamentals required for executing each.

Inbounds Clear

An alert team that converts quickly from defense to offense, with quick ball movement and efficient player positioning, can often generate either fast or slow break scoring opportunities off an inbounds clear. (See Chapter Nine, "The Transition Game.") A typical inbounds clear occurs following a goalie save. Immediately after securing possession of the ball, the goalie will alert his team defense with a "Break" or "Clear" call. The closest defender in the vicinity of the shooter (M_3 in the diagram) anticipates the save and breaks upfield, looking over his shoulder for an outlet pass. M_4 also breaks upfield as a possible release. M_5 should delay his break and drift toward the sideline in anticipation of a possible weak-side safety-valve pass. The midfielders should always be conscious of spreading out as they break upfield. This spread pattern makes it difficult for one rider to cover two people, and also assists the goalie in locating an open teammate to receive the outlet pass.

The two wing defensemen, D_1 and D_2, break upfield and toward the sideline on a "banana" type route, looking over their outside shoulder for a

Inbounds Clearing

Many excellent scoring opportunities begin with the goalie's outlet pass. In this sequence, the goalie prepares to stop a shot on goal (A). After making the save, he quickly looks upfield (B). He passes to a teammate who, the moment the save was made, instantly switched from defense to offense (C).

The inbounds clear.

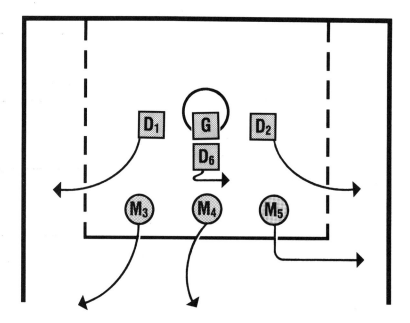

clearing pass. D_6 should protect the crease area and provide an immediate safe outlet for the goalie if he cannot locate a teammate upfield.

After a save, the goalie directs the clear. Excellent scoring opportunities often originate with a well executed outlet pass from the goalie to a teammate breaking upfield. The goalie should first look to the direction of the shot. However, he should also be sure to take a few seconds to scan the entire field for other possible outlet opportunities upfield. By the rules of lacrosse, a goalie has four seconds, after making a save, to make a pass or leave the circle. Failure to do either in four seconds results in awarding possession of the ball outside the restraining box to the opposition. As the four second time allotment approaches, and the goalie has not found an outlet, he should exit either the side or back of the crease, and D_6 should move towards the goalie to provide a possible release. It's important that the three midfielders and two wing defensemen maintain eye contact with the ball as they break upfield. If the goalie exits through the side or back of the crease, everyone must be aware of his move, and thereupon discontinue moving upfield, and break back toward the ball.

The clearing team enjoys a numerical advantage in the defensive half of should try to create a situation that forces one of the six riders (more on riding later) to defend two clearers.

Out-of-Bounds Clear

An out-of-bounds clear follows any official stoppage of play and subsequent awarding of possession to the defense. The offense can turn the ball over to the defense by passing the ball out-of-bounds, stepping on either sideline or the endline while in possession, or having the ball leave the field of play following a stick or body check. Failure to properly back up a shot, as well as any technical foul assessed against the offense, will also result in possession being awarded to the defense. Clearing from out-of-bounds involves considerably more strategy with respect to player alignment and patterns of movement than inbounds clears.

The goalie, close defensemen, and midfielders can position themselves in a number of alignments when clearing from the endline. Clearing alignments from the endline can be identified by using a simple numbering system. Starting with the endline and moving upfield to the midline, the numbers coincide with the relative position of the seven members of the clearing team. For example, a three-one-three formation aligns three clearers along the GLE, one upfield at the restraining line, and three across the midline. Let us examine a few basic clearing alignments and the strategy that accompanies each.

Three-One-Three

This alignment, as diagrammed, is often referred to as an "L" clear. Two defensemen (D_1 and D_2) position themselves on either side of the goalie, outside the restraining box, along the GLE. The "L" defenseman (D_6) aligns along the sideline, at the midline. The "L" defenseman can position himself to either side of the field, and M_5 will adjust his alignment accordingly. M_5 assumes a position at the midline on the opposite side of the field as the "L" defenseman (D_6). M_3 and M_4 stack in the center of the field with M_3 at the face-off "X" and M_4 directly in front, near the restraining line.

Either wing defenseman (D_1 or D_2) handles the ball as it is put into play along the endline. The goalie remains in the crease, available for a pass behind the goal. If the riding team attempts to deny the goalie the ball behind the goal, he may break out the front door to receive a release pass upfield.

M_3 and M_4 work together in tandem to find soft spots or voids in the ride.

The 3-1-3 out-of-bounds clear.

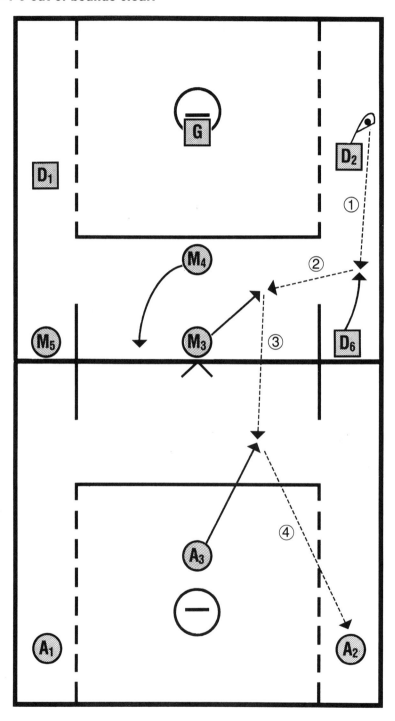

The offense enjoys a seven versus six player advantage and should force one rider to defend two members of the clearing team. M_5 and D_6 work along the sideline in anticipation of a possible release pass. As the ball swings toward the sideline, M_5 or D_6 may break down for the ball or upfield over the midline. If M_5 or D_6 receives the ball while moving back toward the endline, he should look immediately to M_3 or M_4, breaking upfield. Care should be taken not to force the ball. Patience and high percentage passes are the key. If a teammate cannot be located upfield, do not hesitate to pass the ball back and redirect it to the other sideline. Anytime D_6 breaks over the midline, the far side midfielder (M_5) must be alert to stay onside.

The three attackmen in the offensive goal area are key participants in any clearing effort. As a general rule, A_1 and A_2 align along either sideline deep in the offensive half of the field, just above the GLE. From this position, A_1 or A_2 can receive long, high-arcing clearing passes, or break quickly upfield to provide a release for teammates as they cross the midline. From his position in the center of the field, A_3 assumes a more active role in the clear. By anticipating and timing his move, A_3 can break upfield at key times to receive clearing passes from teammates in the defensive half of the field.

Four-Across Clear

Many teams align a midfielder alongside the goalie, creating a four across clear. From this position the midfielder (M_3) handles the ball as it is put into play from the endline, taking advantage of his open field dodging and passing skills. This clear is particularly effective against pressure rides.

As seen in the diagrams, the remaining three members of the clearing team (M_4, M_5, and D_6) assume one of two basic alignments. The four-three alignment allows M_3 to maneuver up the middle of the field, looking to run by a single rider or, when confronted with a double-team, to pass the ball to an open teammate. A four-one-two formation, with M_4 aligning near the restraining line, allows more immediate midfield support. M_3 and M_4 can work together to create a two-on-one situation as the ball is exchanged along the sideline between the goalie, D_1, and D_2. In both four-across clears (the four-three and the four-one-two), M_5 and D_6 align the same, upfield and toward the sideline, with M_5 always assuming a position on the same side of the field as M_3, and with D_6 in the opposite corner.

As M_3 advances the ball upfield, it is important that the goalie and the two wing defensemen (D_1 and D_2) maintain a proper position in relation to him. By staying even with, or slightly ahead of the ball, the two wing defense-

The four-across clear: 4-3 alignment.

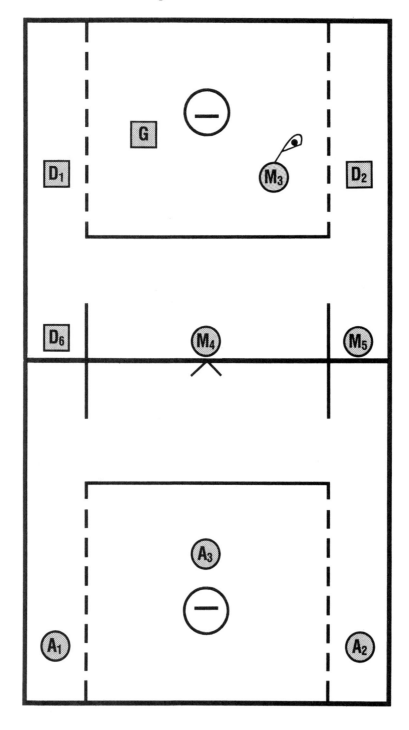

The four-across clear: 4-1-2 alignment.

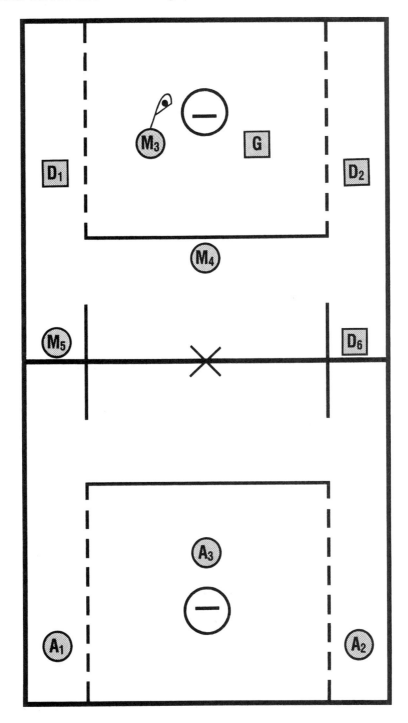

men can be more easily located by M_3 in the event he is under pressure and must find a release. The goalie remains a few yards behind M_3 as he maneuvers upfield. From this position, M_3 can always pass the ball back to the goalie, who may then redirect the ball to either wing defenseman to make a pass upfield.

Sideline Clear

Any time the defense is awarded possession upfield between the restraining line and the midfield line, an excellent opportunity exists for a quick clear and a transition goal. As seen in the diagram, aligning all three midfielders to one side of the field provides a variety of clearing options. By looking directly down the sideline, M_3 has a choice of passing to M_4, near the midline, M_5, near the far restraining line, or A_2, in the deep corner.

With two midfielders aligned in the defensive half of the field, D_1 and D_2 are free to break over the midline and receive a pass directly from either M_3 or the goalie. This option can result in a transition scoring opportunity for the clearing team.

If M_3 cannot locate a release upfield, the goalkeeper can provide immediate assistance. Quite often a return pass from the goalie to M_3 will present the midfielder with an opportunity to run the ball out of the defensive half of the field.

Failure to consistently clear the ball can quickly frustrate and demoralize a team. Broken clears normally catch the defense out of position and make them vulnerable to quick goals following turnovers.

Keeping in mind a few key points will greatly assist your clearing efforts. Staying spread out forces defenders to ride the entire field. At the same time, the soft spots or voids will become more obvious to the clearing team. Whenever possible, two members of the clearing team should look to isolate one rider. Staying spread out greatly facilitates locating and taking advantage of a two on one situation.

Consistently effective clearing teams are alert at the midfield line. The responsibility for achieving proper player balance and staying onsides rests with the midfielders. As a general rule, the midfielder or midfielders farthest from the ball are responsible for staying onside when necessary.

Keeping your eye on the ball is also very important. This basic concept keeps everyone alert, ready to move into open areas, or to provide a release for a teammate with the ball. Anticipation and timing are key elements for members of the clearing team as they move into open areas of the field to receive a pass. Try to anticipate the clearing pattern and time the break when your

A sideline clear.

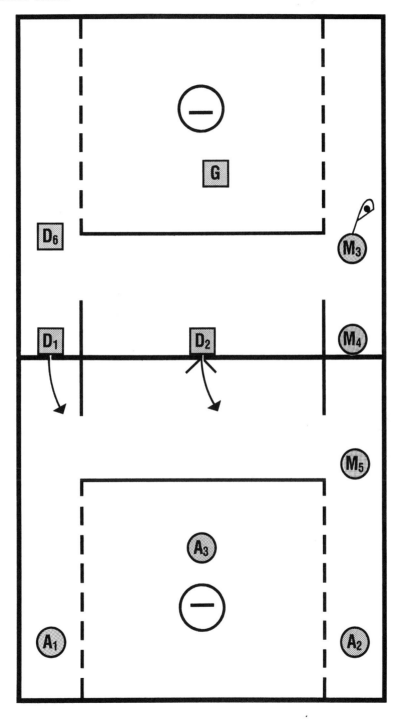

Successful offensive teams are always enthusiastic.

teammate with the ball is in good position to make a pass. When breaking back toward your own goal to receive a clearing pass, be sure to move to meet the ball and make a big turn toward the sideline. Make all passes on the move and be constantly aware of advancing the ball by running in open areas or passing to teammates open upfield. Avoid directing clearing passes to the area in front of the goal.

Successful clearing requires the proper combination of push and patience. Letting the ball do the work by pushing or passing it upfield can result in transition scoring opportunities. There are situations, however, that require patience, good judgment, and respect for the ball. Repetition and drill work help your team to recognize when it is advantageous to push the ball upfield quickly, or to pull it back and clear the ball with patience and control. Concentration and repetition are the keys to effective clearing.

SUMMARY

In order to generate a good scoring opportunity, team offensive movement must be understood and executed crisply by all six players. As we will see in Chapter Six, "Extra-Man Offense," and Chapter Nine, "The Transition Game," it is considerably easier for the offense to receive a high-percentage shot when a numerical advantage over the defense exits. All-even, or six-on-six, offense requires precise execution by unselfish players willing to set picks, screen the goalie, back up the goal, and move intelligently without the ball. All-even offense presents a real challenge that teams must meet with hard work and constant attention.

6

Extra-Man Offense

Whenever a time-serving penalty is committed, the fouled team is awarded possession at the midline (if the penalty occurred in the defensive half of the field) or outside the attack goal area (if the penalty occurred in the offensive half of the field). An extra-man offensive advantage (six offensive players versus five defenders) is now in effect for the fouled team. Similar to the hockey power play, extra-man offense (EMO) provides the fouled team with an excellent opportunity to work for a high-percentage shot.

Most goals in lacrosse are scored when the offensive team enjoys a numerical advantage over the defense. The transition game (discussed in Chapter Nine) and extra-man offense are the usual ways the offense can gain a numerical advantage. It's important, therefore, that your team understand and take full advantage of each extra-man offensive opportunity.

Extra-man offense allows lacrosse teams to showcase their best offensive players. These EMO units must be well drilled and capable of moving the ball quickly and efficiently for a high percentage shot. A realistic team goal for the EMO unit is to score on at least 35 percent of its opportunities. Most teams can count on anywhere from six to ten penalties a game. Therefore, a two- to three-goal difference may depend on the EMO proficiency. To achieve this level of success, EMO must be practiced regularly. The players must be able to anticipate each other's movements and to develop a sense of unity and pride.

The players who combine the best stick skills (passing and shooting) with good field sense should be selected for the EMO unit. If possible, the unit should have a healthy mixture of good outside shooters, inside players, one good feeder, and at least one natural left-hander. The ideal breakdown is to have three attackmen and three midfielders on the EMO unit, though it is quite possible that four attackmen and two midfielders will make up the extra-man

127

Extra-man offense situations frequently lead to high-percentage shots on goal.

unit. In this case, one attackman must be alerted to play as a midfielder in the event the ball is lost and cleared over the midline. One year at Hobart, our EMO team had five midfielders and one attackman. We had to constantly remind two of the middies to stay back on the attack half of the field to satisfy the offside rule.

If you're a coach, personnel selection is a primary consideration when formulating your EMO philosophy. If your team is blessed with a couple of excellent outside shooters, you can afford to be less structured and more free-wheeling. Some teams, however, must be very disciplined and execute a number of passes and cuts to ultimately achieve the shot they feel they can convert for a goal. Teams that rely heavily on set plays should be flexible enough to recognize, and to take advantage of, defensive breakdowns whenever they occur. Likewise, freelancing EMO teams (ones that do not rely on structured patterns) should have a few dependable set plays they can fall back on, if necessary.

As a coach, you should be sure that there are a few options available in every set play you design. There is plenty of opportunity for creativity. At least four additional players should work with your regular EMO unit to provide backup support in the event of an injury. Some teams have had success with two separate EMO units. Each unit may have a special play or two in addition to three common plays. Having two separate units gets more players involved, is great for morale, and also provides a practice team to work against your penalty killing, or man-down defensive unit.

MAXIMS

Before we examine the common EMO formations and a few basic plays, let's review some individual and team maxims for effective extra-man play.

Individual

1. Stay wide to help spread out your opponent's defense, and to open up the passing and cutting lanes.

2. Do not stand still. Instead, move your feet, and pass sharply *to the outside* (important, as we shall see).

3. Back up all shots and feeds.

4. Do not hold the ball too long; occasionally reverse the direction you throw the ball, or bypass a man with your passes.

5. Do not allow one defender to play two people.
6. Be alert to know how much time is left in the penalty.
7. Screen the outside shots and be alert for rebounds.
8. Get a good shot every time.

Team

1. Be patient, particularly when operating with a one minute penalty. Let the ball do the work.
2. Practice your EMO "skeleton," or formation, without a defense, as well as against a live defense.
3. Be flexible; know all the options off a set play.
4. Put a stopwatch on the penalties in practice so the EMO unit develops a sense of timing.
5. Have a quick play (10 seconds) rehearsed.
6. Be prepared if the defense shuts a man off; that is, denies a man the ball by closely face-guarding him.
7. Be prepared for a two-man-up situation (six attackers versus four defenders).
8. Be alert to ride hard after a change of possession, shut off the goalie, and put your best rider on the ball.

FORMATIONS AND PLAYS

Like the all-even offensive alignments discussed in the previous chapter, extra-man offensive formations are identified by the number of players in the midfield, across the crease area, and behind the goal. A team that aligns in a two-three-one has two players in the midfield, three across the crease, and one behind the goal.

A few college teams blessed with great outside shooters are content to align in one of the various formations and work for a shot by moving the ball quickly around the perimeter, occasionally bypassing a man. They may try to connect with an attackman moving around the goal from behind for a quick shot on the edge of the crease. This maneuver, known as a "sneak," can be very effective if timed properly.

Most teams, however, approach extra-man offense with a philosophy that involves more player movement. Considerably more pressure can be placed on the man-down defense if the offense changes formations. Voiding areas with cuts and filling these voided areas with constant movement can keep the man-down off balance, confused, and out of position. Carefully designed off-ball movement coordinated with crisp pass work can often result in a wide-open shot on the front door of the goal.

Let's take a look at some basic EMO formations and plays.

The Three-One-Two

The three-one-two alignment is an excellent place to start when teaching EMO. From this formation, players can move to a variety of other alignments and in effect disguise the EMO play.

As seen in the diagram of the three-one-two play, the ball is passed around the perimeter in a clockwise direction. The ball can go around the horn a few times before the play is set into motion by a predetermined "Go" or "Get it" call.

Phase One As A_1 is about to receive the ball from M_3, A_6 establishes a high post and M_5 makes a diagonal left-handed cut toward the ball. A_1 gives the cutter a quick look and will feed him if he is open.

Phase Two If he does not make the feed, A_1 quickly passes across to A_2. M_3 anticipates this pass and simultaneously makes a right-handed cut to the ball. A_2 looks quickly to the cutter and feeds if he is open.

Phase Three As M_3 makes his cut, M_4 rolls a few steps to his right in anticipation of a pass from A_2. M_4 moves into the ball, gathering momentum for a well-screened outside shot.

Phase Four If M_4 elects not to shoot, he immediately looks to M_5 who has curled up away from the goal with his stick to the outside. Upon receiving the pass from M_4, M_5 immediately dumps the ball to A_1 sneaking around from behind. A_2 moves behind to back up the goal and provide a release, if necessary. If A_1 does not have a shot, he will pass to A_2 at the point behind the goal. M_3 has moved out to the wing, and M_5 has joined A_6 on the crease. We are now in a one-four-one alignment with M_4 up top.

The one-four-one formation can put considerable pressure on the man-down defense. There are two immediate scoring threats on the crease (M_5 and A_6). They also are in excellent position to screen an outside shot from up top (M_4), or either wing area (A_1 or M_3). A_2, behind the goal, is in excellent position to feed, back up shots, or *sneak* around either side of the goal.

A basic 3-1-2 EMO play.

Phases 1 through 3.

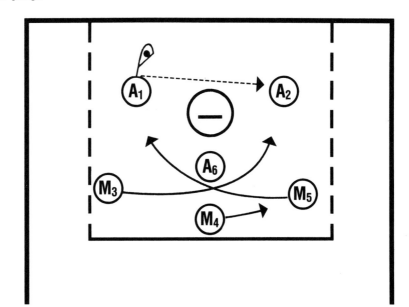

Phase 4.

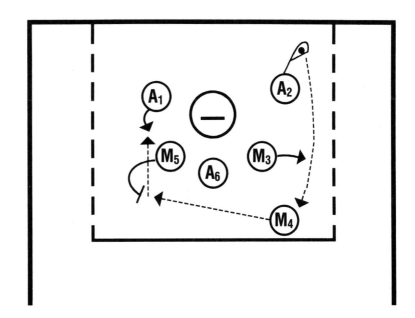

The Two-Three-One

The two-three-one is a common EMO formation. The attackman behind the goal functions like a point guard in basketball, distributing the ball to open teammates. He can also be a scoring threat by sneaking around either side of the goal. The two-three-one is well suited for cutting plays as well as outside shots.

The two-three-one play diagrammed here is basic, but effective, if run with the proper timing.

Phase One The ball moves clockwise around the perimeter. As the ball is passed from M_3 to A_1, M_5 cuts across the goal to the ball. A_6 positions at the midpoint of the goal and curls to the ball as M_5 cuts by. A_1 looks inside quickly to feed either M_5 or A_6.

A basic 2-3-1 EMO play.

Phase 1.

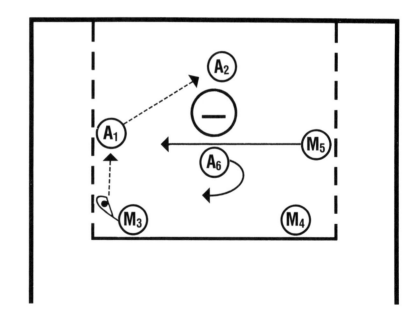

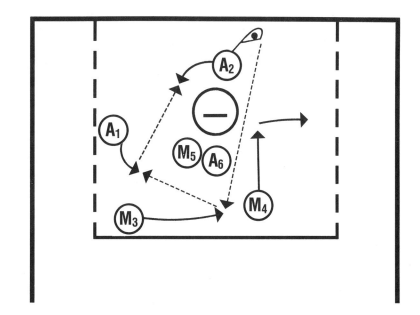

Phases 2
through 4.

Phase Two If he does not make a feed inside, A_1 immediately passes the ball to A_2 positioned at the point, behind the goal. M_4 anticipates this pass to the point and makes a straight right-handed cut down the goal pipe. A_2 looks to feed this cut.

Phase Three As M_4 cuts to the goal, M_3 rolls to his right, filling the voided area up top. If he does not feed the cutter, A_2 passes to M_3 for a possible outside shot. After completing his cut down the pipe, M_4 slides out to the wing area. M_5 and A_6 occupy the crease area.

Phase Four After looking to shoot, M_3 passes to A_1 rolling up toward the midfield area. A_1 receives the ball to the outside and looks to immediately feed A_2, who has come from the far side of the goal for a right-handed shot on a "sneak." This play also ends in a one-four-one alignment. From the one-four-one, the EMO can continue to pass the ball quickly around the perimeter, occasionally skipping a man, looking for a good shot. It's also helpful to redirect the ball occasionally, or pass it back, rather than always moving it in one direction.

The One-Four-One

Many EMO plays will culminate in a one-four-one alignment. This formation puts maximum pressure on the defense with two screeners or shooters on the crease and three shooters spread from wing to wing. The one-four-one is a popular short-time play formation. In the one-four-one play diagrammed, the two crease attackmen align 8 to 10 yards above the crease and in a tandem position.

Phase One The ball moves counterclockwise around the horn. As A_1 receives the pass from M_5, A_6 makes a right-handed cut down the pipe.

A basic 1-4-1 EMO play.

Phases 1
and 2.

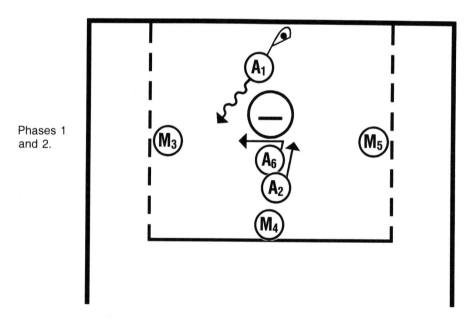

Phase Two A_1 carries the ball to his right, forcing the goal, looking to shoot, if possible. A_6 switches the stick to his left hand and slides across the front of the goal to the left pipe. A_2 simultaneously cuts down the right pipe for a right-handed shot. A_1 looks to feed inside to either A_6 or A_2.

A basic 1-4-1 EMO play (cont).

Phase 3.

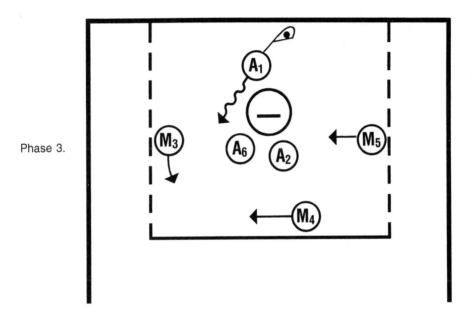

Phase Three As A_1 moves to his right, M_5 slides in from the wing area for a back-door feed on the weak side, away from the ball. M_3 rolls up and M_4 moves to his left. A_1 must now read the situation as he approaches the GLE. His choices are: feed M_5 on back door, feed M_4 for an outside shot, feed M_3 for a midrange shot, or keep coming around for a shot.

The Three-Three

In recent years the three-three has become a very popular EMO formation. Since all six offensive players are in position to shoot, maximum pressure is placed on the defense. Backing up shots can be difficult from this alignment. The midfielder in the M_4 position serves as the quarterback. He must be able to recognize where the defense is vulnerable and make the appropriate feed to take advantage of the situation.

A well-orchestrated EMO unit can move very easily from the three-three alignment into almost any other formation, putting added pressure on the defense. If the offense elects to sit in the three-three, it's imperative that one defender not be allowed to play two people.

Man-down defenses usually try to defend the three-three in one of two ways. They may try to split or play the three top midfielders with two defenders, relying on wing support if necessary, or they may rotate a close defenseman straight up off the crease to assist the two top defenders. Each defensive scheme opens up distinct scoring opportunities for the EMO unit. Needless to say, it's important that every offensive player recognize the defensive scheme being used and react accordingly.

Against a team that attempts to split and play with zone qualities, the EMO must draw in toward the goal, forcing defensive pressure, and then dump the ball to adjacent open attackers. Teams that string or rotate off the crease often leave one of the two low attackmen (A_1 or A_2) open. M_4 must be able to complete passes to the corners, or to the crease man (A_6), popping up near the goal for the ball.

A

B

C

The 3-3 EMO

The 3-3 extra-man alignment shown here is an excellent freelance formation. The defense is packed in very tight (A), so the ball is moved around the perimeter and the shot is taken from the outside (B,C). Note player #10 moving toward the endline to back up the shot (C).

The 3-3 EMO against a team that tries to split and play zone.

A₁ and A₂ play low.

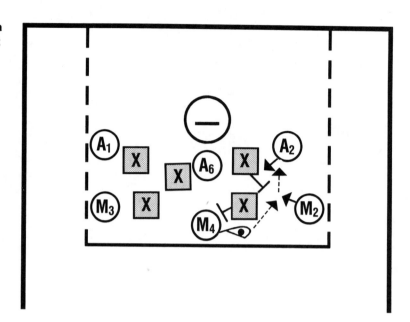

M₄ can pass to A₁ or A₂, or to A₆, who pops up near the goal for the ball.

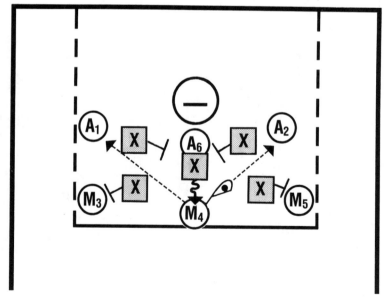

SPECIAL SITUATIONS

One of the unique aspects of lacrosse, when compared to other team sports, are the rules related to shots that leave the field of play. The team closest to the point at which the ball leaves the playing field is awarded possession. Alert offensive teams that position themselves well and anticipate attempts to score can maintain possession of the ball if the shot is not on goal and travels out of bounds. Thus, backing up *all* scoring attempts is extremely important for your EMO unit.

It's quite common for an EMO team to be in possession after a shot with only a short time remaining on the penalty. Teams should practice and be ready to execute a short-time play that will yield a quick opportunity to score.

It's also important that the EMO be ready to take advantage of a two-man-up situation, when the opponent's defense loses two men temporarily to penalties. In this situation, one man behind the goal is all that is necessary to allow both maximum offensive pressure, and the adequate backing-up of wide shots. A well-prepared EMO team will also know how to respond if the defense elects to shut off, or deny, one man the ball. The offensive man who is being denied the ball should either go to the crease or stand on the perimeter and allow the EMO to work five vs. four.

It's a privilege to be selected to play extra-man offense. Patience, pride, and persistence are the keys. Always work for the best possible shot, but don't be discouraged if your team doesn't score every time.

7

Team Defense

Every successful lacrosse team must develop a coordinated team defense that is capable of reacting to a variety of offensive plays and setups. The individual defensive skills discussed in Chapter Four must be combined to allow the goalie, the three close defensemen, and the three midfielders to work together as a *team* defensive unit. Successful teams develop great pride in their defense. A team's offensive production can be adversely affected by poor weather, a bad shooting day, or a mild slump, but defense must be consistent.

The immediate objective of the defense is to *prevent the opposition from scoring.* To realize this objective, the defense must control the offense, limit the high percentage shots, put the ball on the ground, gain control, and clear the ball to its own offense. Team defenses that communicate and anticipate well will quickly develop the pride and cohesion necessary for success.

DEFENSIVE TERMINOLOGY

The goalie leads the team defense by periodically pinpointing the location of the ball with a strong clear voice command. Some teams standardize their terminology by labeling the areas around the goal with numbers, using the same ones for offense and defense. A one-through-six system, where the goalie calls out the number of the ball's location, is common. Ball location can also be pinpointed by using clock reference points with the goalie facing directly out at twelve o'clock. Perhaps the most common directional commands actually describe the ball location: "front right," "back left," etc. Defenders must discipline themselves to tune in to the goalie's voice so they are always aware of ball location.

141

Effective team defenses anticipate and communicate.
Defenders must always be prepared to provide support
for one another.

Identifying Defensive Zones

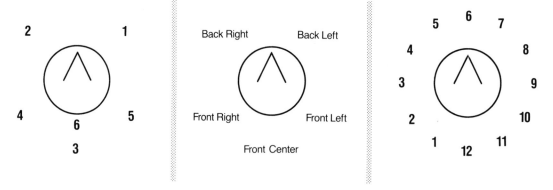

Defensive zones and ball location can be identified by using a 1 through 6 numbering system (left), descriptive terminology (center), or clock reference points (right).

To facilitate defensive coordination, the areas around the goal are identified as *crease, hole, perimeter,* and *point.* The *crease* is nine feet in radius. Offensive players are prohibited from entering the crease but defensive personnel may travel through the crease as long as they do not have possession of the ball. Alert defenders quickly learn to use the crease to assist in recovering and reestablishing position on attackmen dodging from behind. After gaining possession of the ball in the crease, the goalie has four seconds to make a pass or leave the circle. With possession of the ball in the crease, the goalie's stick cannot be checked. However, it is legal to check him after he leaves the crease.

The *hole* refers to the area five yards on either side of the goal and 10 to 12 yards out from the crease. This is a critical defensive reference point. Offensive dodgers entering this area must be driven out, forced to their off hand, or immediately double-teamed. Cutters must be played closely in anticipation of a feed and subsequent "check" call from the goalie. When the ball is loose directly in front of the goal, all defenders in the area must try to "clear the crease" with aggressive body checks, allowing the goalie to play the ball. Alert defenders can legally bump their man into the crease resulting in a technical foul on the offense, and possession of the ball awarded to the defense.

The boundaries of the *perimeter* extend to the restraining line in front of the goal and to the dotted lines of the attack goal area to the sides of the goal. This is the area of *maximum team defensive interaction.* Everyone on defense in the perimeter area must be alert and communicate, anticipate, and work together.

Crease Defenders

Crease defenders must be alert and physical. Here the Virginia defender (center) keeps his head on a swivel and maintains steady contact with his man.

A

B

The *point* refers to the area directly behind the goal. A dodger in this area is particularly dangerous because he can utilize his best moves and come around either side of the goal. Many teams will often set picks for the ball at the point, hoping to confuse the defenders. The term "point" as it applies to the area behind the goal is more often used as an offensive reference mark. There is another area in front of the goal that is also referred to as the point. We will see the significance of this point in the chapter on transition offense and defense (Chapter Nine).

Team defensive areas around the goal.

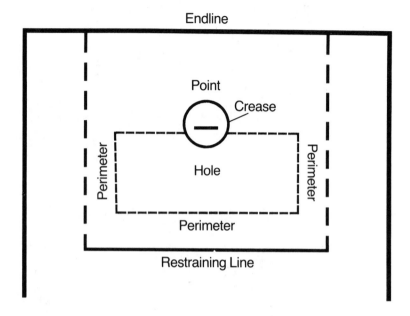

TEAM DEFENSE

All too often, when an offensive player dodges his man and scores a goal, attention is focused solely on the defender who got beat. This is an unhealthy reaction which must be avoided. Teams should think in terms of a seven-man defensive unit (goalie, three defensemen, and three midfielders), and responsibility for defensive lapses should be shared by all seven people. Good team defense is not a series of one-on-one confrontations. It must be a coordinated effort that is conscious of backup support, team defensive slides, and verbal assistance. After a goal is scored, it's wiser for the team defense to focus its attention on who missed the first or second backup slide, rather than pointing the finger at a particular individual. Good team defense is characterized by effective goalie leadership, aggressive controlled pressure on the ball, and alert off-ball anticipation.

There are two basic types of team defense: *man-to-man* and *zone.* Most college teams employ man-to-man as their base defense, but may use some zones in special situations. Teams that elect to play zone defenses exclusively must teach basic man-to-man techniques to those defenders on the ball, and conversely, man-to-man teams should stress zone qualities to the defenders off the ball. The main focus here will be man-to-man defense which incorporates zone qualities off the ball.

Defense On the Ball

The defender on the ball has a dual responsibility. He must be under control to minimize penalties and to prevent situations where he is easily dodged, and at the same time he must be aggressive enough to discourage high-percentage shots and uncontested feeds. The defender on the ball should employ the fundamental footwork and basic stick checks discussed in Chapter Four. He must always work to stay between his man and the goal and be ready to "hold" (see page 90), or to drive his man away from the goal if he enters the hole area.

By continuously listening to the goalie, the defender on the ball can keep his bearings and maintain a clear mental image of where his man is in relation to the goal. The goalie can also provide valuable assistance by directing the defender on the ball to "square right" or "square left," thus adjusting and maintaining good body position.

Poke checks are the order of the day. They should be used in volume to keep the attacker's bottom hand off the stick and to prevent him from facing the goal. As a defender on the perimeter senses his man is about to release a pass, he should make an attempt to get that last poke check in—then immediately step back and get involved in the team defensive responsibilities for an off-ball defender. This step backward will help him to avoid getting beat on a give-and-go, and also ensure good off-ball position.

Defense Off the Ball

Defenders off the ball, on the perimeter, use zone techniques to ensure proper team defensive reaction. By sagging or dropping off their man and playing "heavy," or toward the ball, the perimeter defenders will be in good position to cover cutters, clog the passing lanes, and provide backup support for the defender on the ball. Alert off-ball defenders keep their sticks up to discourage passes through the hole area.

Defenders off the ball must constantly be aware of their body position with respect to ball location and their man. Swiveling your head and placing your body in the best possible position to "see the ball, see your man" is very important. Each off-ball defender on the perimeter should be able to form an imaginary triangle connecting himself with the ball and his man. Peripheral vision is a tremendous help.

Defenders at the midfield should always stay between their man and the goal. When the ball is in the midfield, the defenders who are guarding men behind the goal should play a few yards above the GLE. Good off-ball position is very important. In general, the farther your man is from the ball, the more you should sag. Remember to keep your head on a swivel, that is, alternating between the ball and your man.

Off-ball defenders on either side of a teammate guarding the ballcarrier should provide verbal assurances that they are in good position to assist. "Back-left" or "Back-right" calls indicate to the man defending the ballcarrier that defensive support is imminent. Adjacent defenders are in excellent position to assist on loose balls, knock shooters down, call out picks, or provide backup support. As the ball is passed around the perimeter, the backup support should reidentify itself.

DEFENSIVE SLIDES (BACKUP)

Defenders adjacent to the ball must be alert to provide backup support in the event the man guarding the ballcarrier needs help. You cannot hesitate to leave your man if a team defensive slide is needed. By sagging off your man heavy to the ball, you will be in good position to slide from the inside out. Anticipation is the key to a successful backup. *Slide under control,* with your head up and with your stick covering the dodger's stick. As you approach the shooter, check his stick and lower your shoulder into his chest. It's not necessary to rush out of control at the attacker and attempt to knock him into the hot dog stand. You run the risk of missing, fouling, or getting dodged. The diagrams illustrate a few team defensive slides. Many times a second or even a third slide is necessary as the offense keeps the ball moving. These slides will become much more obvious if the perimeter defenders maintain good off-ball position and antici- pate the play.

A typical defensive slide.* In this situation, the defender, M_4, has just been beaten by a dodge. To answer this offensive move, M_3 makes the first slide, covering the ballcarrier. Meanwhile, D_1 moves up in readiness for a second slide, and D_2 moves across the crease in readiness, if necessary, for a third slide.

*Slide—A move by a defender to give support to a teammate who has been beaten by his man.

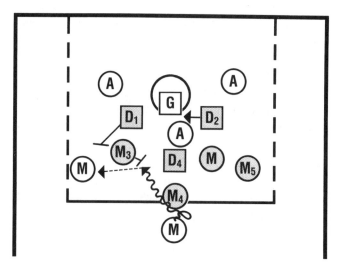

Defensive slide when defender is beaten from behind the GLE.

Here, D_2 is the defender beaten on a dodge from behind the GLE. M_5 makes the first slide down to support. M_4 anticipates a second slide and M_3 a third slide, if necessary.

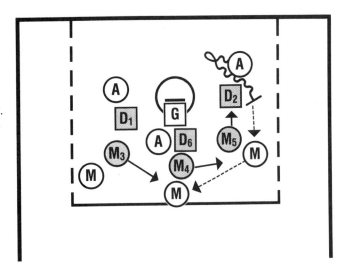

DEFENSE ON THE CREASE

Defenders on the crease are faced with a different role than those on the perimeter. Offensive players positioned on the crease are an immediate threat to score. Therefore, *they must receive constant close attention.* There will be occasions when a team defensive slide from the crease is necessary. However, for the most part, crease defenders will stay at home (that is, near the crease). Not only do you leave a man open in prime scoring territory, but also, it's difficult to anticipate a defensive slide off the crease. To play effective crease defense, the defender must center his concentration totally on the offensive player. You cannot afford the luxury of splitting your attention between your man and the ball.

All defensive players are potential creasemen and should learn to play in front of the goal. Crease defenders may have their backs to the ball on occasion; therefore, tuning in to the goalie's commands is especially important. The crease can become a very congested area and it's necessary for defenders to keep their sticks in an upright position. That will facilitate moving through traffic and will allow the crease defender (or defenders) to chop-check down on an attacker's stick quickly and without a windup (see page 88, "The Chop Check").

Communication between teammates is critical when playing defense on the crease. Picks must be identified early and teammates should talk and guide each other through traffic. Whenever possible, get through the pick, or between your teammate and the pick, avoiding a switch unless absolutely necessary. The

A

Fighting Through a Pick

In this sequence, the offensive
player (in white) on the right
tries to free his teammate for
a shot on goal by setting a
pick on #24 (A,B,C). But #24
spots the pick (B), fights
through it (C), and stays with
his man (D).

B

C

D

Switching Men on a Pick

Here, when the offensive player (in white) on the right sets a pick on #24 (A,B,C), #10 calls "Switch!" and picks up #24's man (D).

A

B

C

D

defender playing the pick man will do most of the talking. It's his responsibility to warn his teammate of the approaching pick and to allow him space to slide through. If a "Switch" call is necessary, the defender playing the pick man makes the call, clearly giving his teammate ample time to react and pick up a new man.

The crease defender's position relative to his man will vary according to the location of the ball and the location of the crease attackman. When the ball is behind the goal in the prime feeding areas and the crease attacker is in a low post position, the defender should play no more than two feet from his man. If you are the crease defender, try to stay between your man and the ball, but *do not get too preoccupied with the ball.* Keep your stick on the side of the attacker's stick, ready to check down quickly on the head of the stick or on the attacker's upper arm.

As the crease attackman moves to a high post (5 to 10 yards above the crease, the crease defender's cushion should increase. Maintain good body position between the attacker and the ball. By using your bottom hand as a feeler placed on the offensive man's hip, you can steal a peek at the ball.

Any time the ball is in the midfield, a crease defender should play with a slight cushion (one to two yards) in front of his man. By utilizing split vision, the crease defender can anticipate any slide he may be called on to make.

Crease defenders must try to prevent the goalie from being screened. Screens are a fact of life on the crease, but the defense can keep them to a minimum by rerouting screeners with subtle yet firm hip checks.

ZONE DEFENSE

In the past few years, the zone defense has undergone a bit of a resurgence, particularly at the secondary level. Zone defenses can unnerve and create problems for the offense, and, as we've seen, teams that play good man-to-man defense actually adhere to zone principles off the ball. Although not as sophisticated as basketball zones, nor as frequently used, zone defenses in lacrosse provide a change of pace and force teams to adjust their offense.

Teams that commit to pure zone defenses do so for a variety of reasons. Zone defenses help to contain strong dodging teams by providing immediate predetermined backup. Offenses must be patient and handle the ball well to successfully penetrate zone defenses. If your defensive personnel are out-manned, but you have a competent goalie, the zone can help your team stay competitive by encouraging the opposition to take outside shots. Zone defenses also stress many of the same principles of man-down defense, (stay tight, keep your sticks up, head constantly on a swivel).

There are weaknesses, or seams, in all zone defenses. Teams must handle the ball well and move intelligently without the ball to exploit these weaknesses. Zone defensive teams must commit additional practice time to ensure proper execution, as coordination and communication must be well rehearsed. Because they tend to be more passive, it's difficult to play catch-up late in a game out of a zone defense.

As the name implies, zone defenses defend men only when they enter predetermined areas. There are many variations and combinations of zone defense; however, the *backer zone* and *perimeter zone* embody characteristics common to most zones.

The *backer zone* predetermines that a single defensive player situated in the middle of the zone back up the man playing the ball. The backer or "monster" aligns between the ball and the goal, three to five yards off the defender playing the ballcarrier. He can slide early and double-team the ball, or assume the role of a quarterback and direct the team slides from his inside position. The backer's alignment in the middle of the defense allows him to identify and call out cutters, as well as anticipate and intercept cross-field passes.

The backer zone.
This zone is useful against teams that lack good outside shooters. The backer (B) is always in position to support the perimeter defender on the ball.

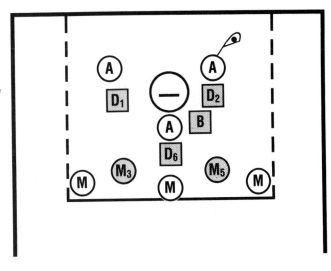

A *perimeter zone* parallels the rotation principles used in a man-down defense. The crease defenseman stays inside, man-to-man, but the remaining five players rotate hard against the flow of the ball. Backside defenders drop way in to provide support on the crease. Increased pressure can be achieved out of this zone by playing the ball aggressively and denying or shutting off the two adjacent release passes.

Recently, some teams have successfully used zones in special situations or as a change-up defense. Zone defenses are successful if they force the offense to make special preparation or to deviate from what they do best.

The perimeter zone. Zone defenses can apply pressure on the ball and be assured of immediate support if needed. The perimeter zone utilizes the same off ball concepts as the rotating man down defense (see Chapter 8).

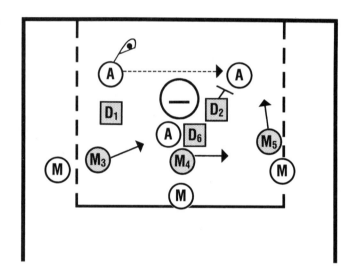

HALLMARKS OF QUALITY TEAM DEFENSE

1. All great teams play great team defense.

2. All seven defenders must share in the successes and setbacks of the defense. Defense is not a series of one-on-one confrontations.

3. Defensive pressure on the ball should be highlighted by good footwork and crisp stick checks. Defense is a healthy blend of body and stick. When in doubt, poke check.

4. Defenders adjacent to the ball must talk and anticipate backup situations. Remember: *See the ball, see the man.*

5. Defensive slides should be well timed and executed from the inside

out, that is, picking up the opponents nearest the goal first, then those on the perimeter of the field. Cover the opponent's stick with your stick, his body with your body. Keep your head up.

6. The farther removed your man is from the ball, the more you should sag (drop off your man toward the crease). However, keep your head on a swivel.

7. Assume a good defensive position and be under control when your man receives the ball in the open field. As he is about to pass, get that last poke check in and immediately step back.

8. Adjust your approach when playing defense on the crease; tighten up, talk, listen for "Check" calls, stay between your man and the ball.

9. Whenever possible, fight through, or slide under, picks, avoiding switching.

10. Communication (listening as well as talking), anticipation, and pride are basic ingredients needed to mold a solid team defense.

RIDING

Whenever the offensive team loses possession of the ball, it must convert quickly to defense in an attempt to disrupt the clear. Riding is the term applied to the defensive efforts directed at regaining possession of the ball. Riding is an extension of team defense, and all players, particularly attackmen, must realize its significance.

Riding incorporates all the individual defensive fundamentals discussed in Chapter Four. By anticipating well, a good riding team can create many turnovers that catch the defense out of position and develop into transition scoring opportunities. Pure fast breaks, slow breaks, three-on-two, two-on-one, or even one-on-one scoring chances can develop, depending on what portion of the field the riding team regains possession of the ball. Teams that are persistent, that hustle, and take pride in their ability to ride can frustrate the opposition. It's impossible for a great offensive team to score if it does not have the ball.

There are a few key principles for attackmen and midfielders to keep in mind when riding:

1. When pursuing an opponent in possession of the ball, take a good angle up the field. Whenever possible, use the sideline as an "extra man" by forcing your opponent out of bounds.

2. Anticipation, hustle, and persistence can make up for lack of speed.

3. Be under control, particularly as you approach an opponent in the open field. Do not overcommit and get beat.

4. When riding the goalie or a long stick defenseman, be aware of check-

Riding

Taking a good angle upfield of your man (A) and checking with an upward motion on his stick (B,C) are just two effective techniques when riding.

A

ing any portion of the butt end of the stick that may be exposed. One-handed wraps or over-the-head checks may be effective. It's also very effective in the open field to check a defenseman's stick up rather than down. It's much more difficult for a long-stick defenseman to absorb the shock of a check up under his stick than a check down on his stick.

5. Take away the sideline route and encourage clearing teams to pass or run the ball toward the middle of the field.

6. Play in zones off the ball, see the ball and any potential clearers in your area. Keep your stick up. Stay within checking range of anyone in your zone, but avoid positioning yourself directly next to an opponent. Defend an area, not just one man.

7. Make the clearing team work. Force them to complete a number of passes in their defensive half of the field. Turn the ball back, away from the midline, whenever possible. Force the clearing team to run or pass *across* the field rather than up the field.

8. Effective communication is necessary to allow an attackman to ride over the midfield line without going offsides. A midfielder must alert the attackman that he is back.

9. After regaining possession of the ball, the riders must make a quick transition back to offense. Look to shoot or to feed a teammate on the crease. Turnovers farther up the field can develop into fast breaks or slow breaks. Be alert and let the ball do the work.

10. Not every riding attempt will be successful. Know when to get back in on defense and concede the clear.

A goalie save or a defensive forced turnover creates an instant, often ad-lib,

B   C

inbounds riding situation. Out-of-bounds situations allow coaches to position their team strategically for more sophisticated and coordinated rides. Nonetheless, both inbounds and out-of-bounds rides can be choreographed and practiced. Let's examine one of each.

Inbounds Ride: The Pinch-and-Run

The term "pinch-and-run" is used to describe the coordinated actions of the offensive team immediately after the opposition goalie saves a shot. In this situation, it's important to make a quick physical and mental transition from offense to defense (riding). By pinching, or containing, the goalie and running quickly upfield, the riding team can prevent the fast break, and then work to achieve a turnover, putting them back on offense.

The first priority for the riding team following a save is to pinch, or prevent the goalie from breaking up the field or completing a quick outlet pass. The crease attackman should position himself on the edge of the crease with his stick up, obstructing the goalie's view and discouraging a quick pass. Maintaining a stick-on-stick position enables the crease attackman to block any direct clearing passes and may ultimately force the goalie to the side or rear of the crease.

In anticipation of outlet passes to the wing defenders, the two remaining wing attackmen should also break upfield and toward the sideline. The riding midfielders must convert quickly from offense to defense by hustling upfield, keeping one eye on the ball, and one eye on any opposition middies breaking into their third of the field.

The Pinch-and-Run: Pinching the Goalie

After a save, alert riding teams "pinch" the goalie—that is, they deny his making a quick outlet pass (A), forcing him to carry the ball to the side (B) or even behind the net (C).

A

B

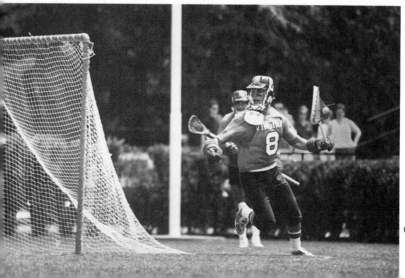

C

Two Pinch-and-Run Clearing Situations

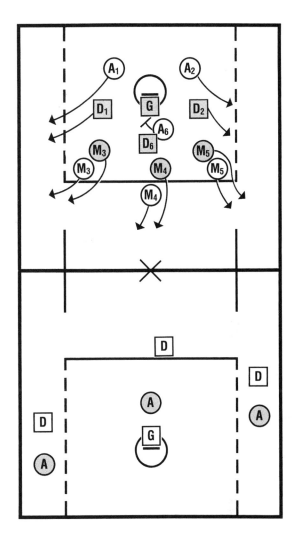

The pinch-and-run clear after a save.

A_6 prevents the quick outlet pass from the goalie, and everyone else hustles upfield to contest the clear.

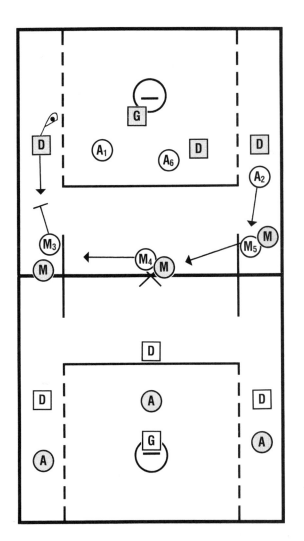

The pinch-and-run: losing containment.

Here, the attack has lost containment, forcing M_3 to slide down and support the ride. M_4 and M_5 slide over, and A_2 drops deep on the weak side.

The defense on the backside of the ride can assist in two ways. First and foremost, they should assume an upfield position (five to eight yards) on their respective attackmen and deny them the ball. It's discouraging for the ride to break down because the defense on the backside did not properly shut off their men. By playing in front of their men, the defense can control the midline. Loose balls that roll over the line or long clearing passes to breaking midfielders can be contested by alert, well-positioned defensemen. The defense is also in good position to direct traffic and to provide valuable verbal assistance to the riding midfielders in front of them.

The farther removed a rider is from the ball, the more he can afford to sag off anyone in his area. After a save, the burden of a ride falls on the three attackmen who are attempting to ride four people (three defensemen and the goalie). There will be times when the clearing defensemen break the riding efforts of the attack. The area between the restraining line and the midline is where the defense normally will gain a clearing advantage. Alert riding midfielders may anticipate this situation and make a coordinated series of slides to check, or turn back, a clearing defenseman. Midfield slides of this type must be well calculated and accompanied by defensive support on the backside of the ride. A deep drop to the midline by the wing attackman, away from the ball side, will also help support the midfield slides.

One of the keys to successful riding is for the attack to hustle upfield whenever a pass is completed over their heads. The midfielder, sliding down, working in coordination with the attack hustling upfield, can create a pinching effect on the opponent.

The Pinch-and-Run: Forcing a Turnover

The riding team can often force a turnover by steering the clearing team to the center of the field, then trapping the ball from both sides.

Out-of-Bounds Ride (Three-Three Zone)

There are a wide variety of strategies riding teams can employ to defend out-of-bounds clearing situations, and by substituting specialized players, coaches can design and implement rides that are highly sophisticated and complex. Out-of-bounds rides can be designed to exert either heavy pressure on the ball by utilizing man-to-man qualities, or minimal pressure on the ball with zone qualities. Each type of ride reflects a different philosophy and can be effective if well executed.

To see some of the salient features of a typical out-of-bounds ride, let's examine a basic three-three, full field zone ride. It is a safe ride that does not allow many transition scoring opportunities. The three-three ride can be used after a save, as well as from an out-of-bounds situation. The zone qualities may help to compensate for a lack of speed on the riding team and at the same time force the clearing team to complete a number of passes.

The purpose of the three-three ride is to jam up the middle of the field and make it difficult for the goalie to pick out an open player. By dropping back toward the midline and allowing the clearing team to come upfield, the defense jams everybody into a small area. The slides become much shorter and the passing lanes can be more effectively defended than if the riding team attempted to cover the entire field.

The attack will be responsible for setting the ride by dropping back to a point approximately five yards above the restraining line. By aligning in a triangle with A_6 at the point, the attack can jam the middle and still effectively cover the width of the field. All riders must have their sticks up, heads on a swivel. Communication among riders is key.

The midfielders divide the width of the field on either side of the midline into thirds. The basic rule is to play the deepest player in the zone. M_4, positioned in the middle of the zone, is a key man. He will make any slides necessary to help the attack. Anytime M_4 is needed to help, the middle zone must be supported by the wing midfielder farthest from the ball. If M_3 slides to the middle, A_1 should drop back to help defend the area vacated by M_3.

The defense on the backside of the ride is once again very important. This is a no-release situation, that is, the defensemen must not allow the completion of a clearing pass to their attackmen. Good upfield position will help the defense to contest the midline and to make any necessary slides in support of the middies.

Zone Rides

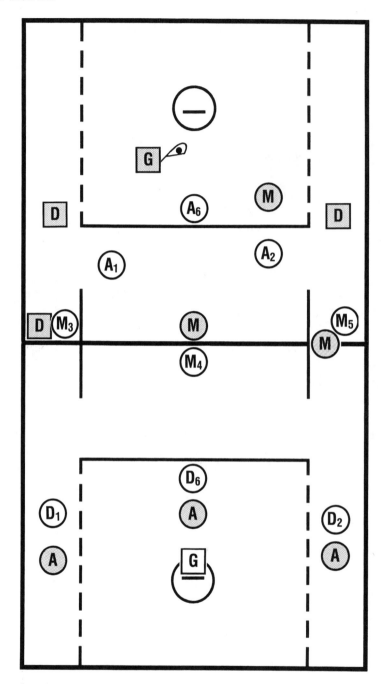

The 3-3, full-field zone ride.

The attack (A_1, A_6, and A_2) must be prepared to move laterally to contain the four across clear.

Zone Rides (Cont.)

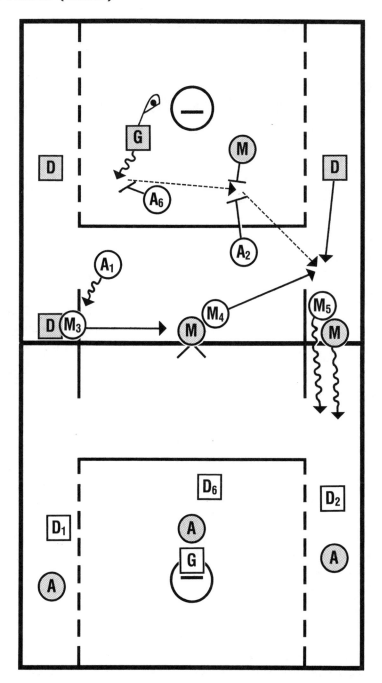

The 3-3, full-field zone ride (cont.)

If the attack loses containment, support must come from the center midfielder (M_4). Here, M_3 slides to support M_4, and A_1 drops toward the midline on the weak side.

**The Out-of-Bounds Ride
(Ten-Man Ride)**

The three-three Zone Ride presents a soft look to the clearing team. The riding team sags back, jams the passing lanes, and traps the ballcarrier upfield between the restraining lines. There will be times when the riding team needs to take the initiative and pressure the clearing team. The Ten-Man or On-Ride relies on pressure and forcing mistakes. The Ten-Man Ride is more risky than the three-three Zone Ride, but it can disrupt the opposition, causing turnovers that can lead to transition scoring opportunities.

As the name implies, the Ten-Man Ride involves the entire team, including the goalie on the backside of the ride. The zone qualities stressed in the three-three ride are replaced by pre-rotated man-to-man pressure. In order to maximize the pressure from the riding team, there will be times when a defenseman on the backside of the ride will cross the midline. Anticipation and communication are essential among the riders aligning along the midline to avoid an offsides penalty.

The riding sequence diagrammed illustrates a Ten-Man Ride against a Four-Across Clear. The attack is pre-rotated to the left side of the field, picking up man-to-man. The attackmen must apply pressure picking up along the GLE.

The midfielders pick up to the right side of the field, the defensemen on the backside align to the left with one man (D_1) riding up at the midline. The goalie completes the pre-rotation by sliding out of the crease area to the right. Whenever possible, the two defensemen (D_2 and D_3) and the goalie slide back and forth on the backside of the ride to try and keep the goalie on the side of the field diagonally opposite from the ball.

As A_2 pressures the ball, M_4 should sag back toward the midline to help support M_5. M_5 must stay onsides to allow D_1 to ride over if necessary. Communication is very important for the riders along the midline.

As the ball is passed over to D_6 along the sideline, A_1 sags back toward the midline to help support D_1. D_1 must stay onsides to allow M_5 to ride over. M_4 anticipates the pass to D_6 and slides down to challenge the ball.

D_2, D_3, and the goalie on the backside of the ride work together to cover the three attackmen. Whenever possible, D_2 and D_3 slide to the ball side and the goalie goes opposite.

Ten-Man Rides require intelligent pressure from the attackmen and midfielders and coordinated midline play among the midfielders and up defensemen. The riders along the GLE must apply enough pressure to discourage long, upfield passes, but they also must not get dodged in the open field.

The 10-Man Ride

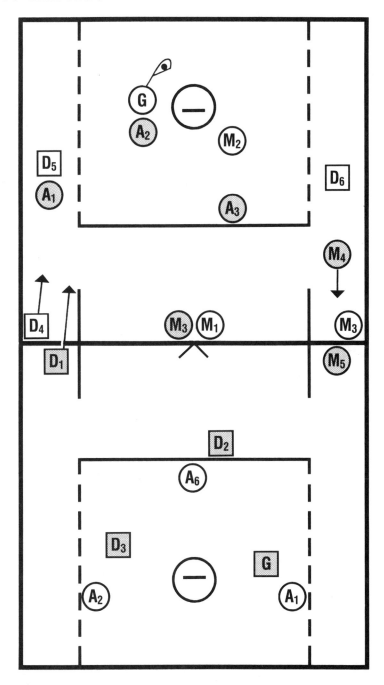

Notice how the players are in position to rotate in the 10-man ride diagrammed here. The attack picks up clearers to the left side, the midfielders pick up clearers to the right, defense to the left, and goalie to the right. M_4 sags back to support M_5 who stays onside to allow D_1 to ride over the midline (A).

The 10-Man Ride (Cont.)

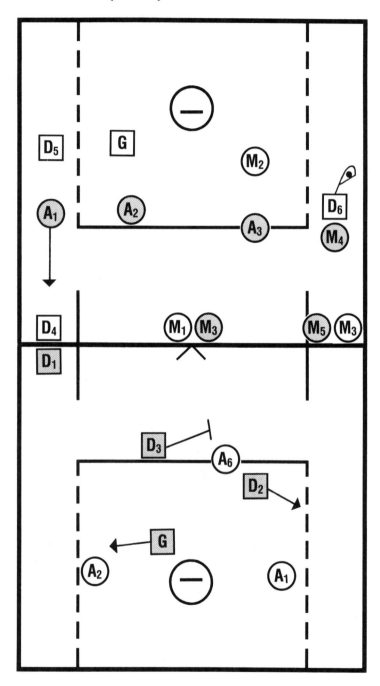

Here, M_4 slides down to challenge D_6. A_1 sags to support D_1 at the midline. Notice the shifting that occurs on the backside of the ride. D_2 and D_3 go to the ball side, and the goalie opposite (B).

There are no shortcuts to effective riding. Every attackman must take pride in his riding ability. Everyone must be sold on its importance and be willing to hustle. The quick transition from offense to defense to offense can result in goals off the ride that can give a team a big boost. Anticipation, communication, and hustle are the key ingredients to developing good riding teams. Remember, it doesn't take a great player to hustle, but all great players do. A team of hustling players makes great riders.

8

Man-Down Defense

MENTAL AND PHYSICAL APPROACH

When faced with playing one man short (for either 30 seconds or one minute), the man-down defensive unit has a great opportunity to swing the momentum of a game. By rising to the occasion and denying the opposition a good scoring opportunity, the man-down defensive unit can provide its team with a tremendous psychological boost. Almost all our big wins at Hobart College have been paved by exceptional man-down defensive performance. Our team goal is to limit the effectiveness of the EMO to 20 percent. Allowing only two goals in every 10 extra-man attempts can provide a tremendous lift for an entire team and at the same time take the wind out of the sails of any opponent.

Successful man-down defenses need great athletes. Mental and physical toughness are essential. Anticipation, quickness (mental and physical), agility, courage, and fierce pride are required as well. The man-down defense (MDD) must communicate effectively and maintain a flexible approach to facilitate adjustments on the fly once the game has begun.

The primary goal of the MDD is to prevent the score. The next objective is to prevent the good shot by containing and directing the offense as to just what it can do. Ultimately, the MDD strives to put the ball on the ground, gain possession, and clear the ball into its own goal area, releasing a teammate from the penalty box. Scoring a shorthanded goal is the ultimate victory for a MDD unit.

MDD incorporates many of the same fundamental techniques used when defending fast breaks. The coordination and teamwork required by effective MDD necessitate constant practice. At least nine players should learn and practice MDD. The traditional makeup of the five-man MDD unit was to have

167

When forced by a penalty to play down a man, the
defense must play as a unit.

three close defensemen team up with two midfielders. The trend in recent years, however, has been to put five "long sticks" (close defensemen) in the game to increase checking range, and, in general, to create more problems for the EMO.

Most teams have the capability of playing two different styles of MDD. A pure *five-man zone,* packed in tight with limited pressure on the ball, is a more passive approach, yet can work well. A *hard-rotation system* attempts to make something happen by pressuring the EMO. Learning to play either style, and mixing them up throughout the course of a game can increase MDD effectiveness. For now, let's look at each.

Areas typically covered in a man-down defensive zone.

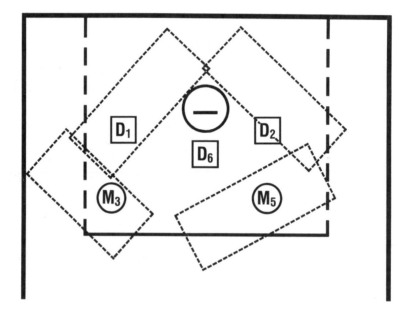

THE FIVE-MAN ZONE (SAFE CALL)

The zone or "safe" call can be effective when a team is unsure what type of extra-man offense it is facing. This style of MDD tests the patience of the offense and often yields only an outside shot. Furthermore, zone, or "safe" MDD is adaptable to a variety of EMO formations.

MDD zones normally start in either a two-one-two or two-three alignment. As in basketball zones, the individual areas of responsibility overlap. The defenders on the perimeter must be quick and clever enough to cover two people. The crease defender relaxes his coverage slightly to assist in identifying and covering cutters. He also is in great position to knock down or intercept passes attempted through the hole area. Backside defenders should always be conscious of sagging inside to help on the crease.

Man-down defense: the 2-1-2.

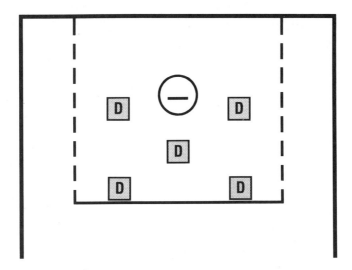

Man-down defense: the 2-3.

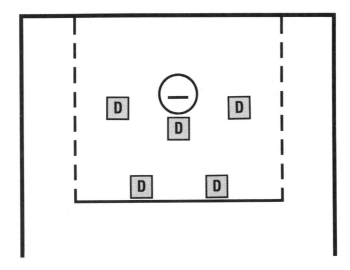

Since zones present a soft look and can appear unthreatening, defenders must put pressure on the ball whenever possible. Poke checks are a must. Off-ball defenders should sag heavily to the ball and *keep their sticks up.* It's every off-ball defender's responsibility to identify and to help cover cutters. The MDD unit must get a feel for which cuts are meaningful and which are merely window dressing. Try not to let the EMO void an area by cutting. It's often possible to share the responsibility of covering cutters as they move through defensive zones. To be successful at "bumping" the coverage of a cutter, the MDD must be super alert and communicate as the cutter moves from one defensive zone to another.

In order for one defender to successfully cover two people, he must adhere to a few basics. If you find yourself asked to play defense in a man-down zone, use the full length of your stick to avoid getting too close to any one offensive player. Keep a wide base and stay on the balls of your feet. Give the man with the ball the impression he is being guarded, when in actuality you are anticipating and mentally moving in the direction of his next pass. Remember, the ball moves faster than you. Save steps whenever you can. Close defensemen may pressure the ball from behind, but care must be taken by the adjacent defensive midfielder to sag down and to cover the voided wing area.

Any zone defender who ventures behind the goal to pressure the ball must hustle back quickly after a pass to rebalance the defensive alignment. Occasionally, the EMO unit will move the ball in such a manner that it forces the MDD to abandon the zone principles and "go" into what, in lacrosse, is known as a rotation. When this happens, everyone must hear the call and react accordingly.

ROTATION ("GO" CALL)

Playing a hard-rotating MDD gets everybody moving and eliminates much doubt and indecision. Man-down defenses that rotate well can disrupt the EMO patterns, force poor passes, and cause turnovers. Anticipation and pressure are the keys.

The basic structure of the rotation positions one man on the ball, one adjacent man on either side of the ball, ready to slide on the next pass, and one man splitting or dividing the distance between the two farthest men from the ball. As in the "safe" call, the crease man stays at home—he does not slide out to double-team—to help direct traffic, and identify cutters. Everyone on the MDD unit must utilize split vision to maintain total awareness of offensive movement.

Rotation ("Go" Call)

Man-down defense: rotation ("go" call), part I.

In a rotation man-down defense, one defender on the ball is always supported by two adjacent teammates. The farthest man from the ball splits his coverage between two opponents.

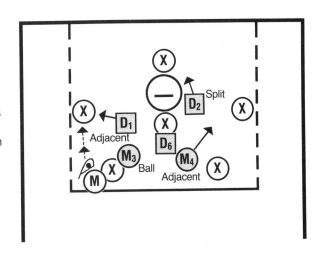

Man-down defense: rotation ("go" call), part II.

As the offense passes the ball around the perimeter, two different defenders become adjacent men and a third becomes the new split man.

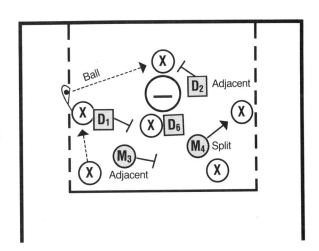

Man-down defense: rotation ("go" call), part III.

The ball has moved to the point man behind the goal. Note how D_2 has rotated to the ball, D_1 and M_4 are adjacent, and M_3 splits his coverage between the two men farthest from the ball.

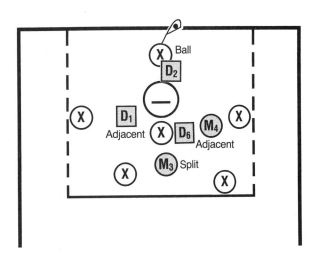

As the ball is passed around the outside of the offensive formation, the four rotating defenders move into, or opposite, the direction of the ball. Every pass around the perimeter changes the role of each rotating defender. As an adjacent defender slides out to play the ball, two new adjacent men are identified, as well as a new split man.

It's imperative for the defender covering a man who has just released the ball to immediately rotate *away* from the pass and back in towards the hole. Resist the temptation to chase the ball—every step toward the ball takes the defender two steps out of position. Keep your eye on the ball but rotate back and away from the direction of the pass.

Coaches should place heavy emphasis on the *form* of the rotation. Rather than rotate in a concentric circle within the offensive formation, the MDD should rotate from inside-out on what appears to be the spokes of a wheel. The spoke concept is critical as it places the off-ball people in excellent inside-out position to cover cutters, intercept passes, and move out at shooters with a good angle.

Proper rotation involves constant movement by the off-ball defenders. The two adjacent defenders and the split man must anticipate and make position adjustments gradually as the ball moves around the horn. Constant and gradual off-ball movement will eliminate the need to rush or lunge at people. Proper body position must be maintained to allow the rotating defenders to see any redirected passes. If the ball is redirected, the rotation must be reversed. The key to a successful man-down rotation is to never relax. The moment the offensive man in your area releases a pass, you must immediately move in the proper direction. Although it can be done, it is not advisable to rotate against certain formations, such as the one-four-one or the three-three. As we shall see, these formations require different man-down defensive strategies.

SPECIAL FORMATIONS AND SITUATIONS

Extra-man offenses that align in either a one-four-one or three-three formation must be given special consideration by the man-down defense. It is difficult to rotate against either formation, although considerable defensive pressure is possible by sliding off the crease.

When defending the one-four-one, the top midfield defender (D_5) is often referred to as the "string man," perhaps because, in this situation, his position demands that he yo-yo up and down the field, as if on a string. His primary responsibility is to work back and forth from the crease area to the top of the

Man-down defensive formation against the 1-4-1.

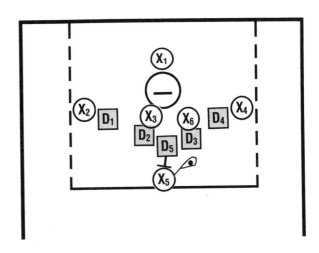

D_5 is the string man. He will sink down toward the crease on a pass from X_5 to either wing (A).

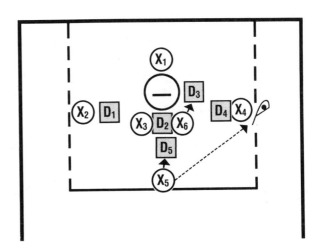

When X_5 passes to X_4, D_4 challenges X_4 on the wing. D_5, on the string, moves down to the crease and tells D_3 he's there (B).

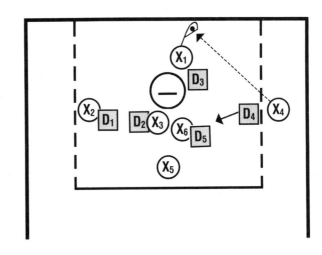

When X_4 passes to X_1, D_5 slides over to cover X_6, releasing D_3 to cover the ball behind the goal. D_4 moves back toward the hole (C).

offensive formation. As the ball is passed from the top center (X_5) to either wing, the string defender begins to sag down toward the crease, anticipating a pass to the point behind. The string man works together with the two defenders on the crease (D_2 and D_3), taking over the position of either of them so that that man is released to pressure the ball at the point. The moment X_1 passes to either wing (X_2 or X_4), the string man (D_5) must start returning to the top center area. Alertness and communication are very important when defending the one-four-one in this manner.

There will be offensive sticks momentarily open on the crease as the ball travels in the air. Crease defenders (D_2 and D_3) should never be in a hurry to leave the hole area to play a man behind the goal. They must *always hustle back* to the crease after defending a man behind the goal. The two wing defenders (D_1 and D_4) sag in to help on the crease whenever they can. Their primary responsibility is defending the wing shooters (X_2 and X_4). The real challenge for a MDD unit is to recognize that the EMO has dropped into a one-four-one, and to adjust accordingly. Communication is a top priority.

The three-three EMO can be defended using a zone (the "safe" call discussed earlier) with the MDD ready to "go" hard (man-to-man), if necessary. With all six offensive players aligned above the goal, it's difficult to use a defensive rotation. However, D_6 can string off the crease to defend X_4. D_3 and D_2 must pinch inside to cover for D_6 any time he leaves the crease to play the midfielder up front. D_3 and D_4 must be conscious of denying the passing lanes between X_4 and the two attackmen on either side of the goal (X_1 and X_2).

Man-down defensive formation #1 against the 3-3: spoking off from the crease.
When the EMO goes into a 3-3 formation, the defense must change. Now the defense spokes off from the crease, with D_6 available to challenge X_4 up top. D_1 and D_2 sag toward the crease, and D_3 and D_4 try to jam the passing lanes between X_4 and X_1 and X_2.

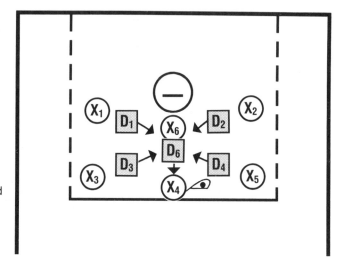

**Man-down defensive
formation #2 against the
3-3: splitting.**

Here, we see the MDD
attempt to "split" the 3-3
EMO. D_3 and D_4 hustle and
anticipate in an effort to
defend the three EMO players
at the top (A).

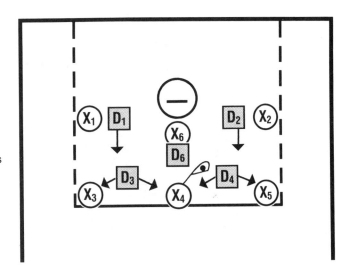

If D_3 and D_4 lose
containment, D_2 must slide up
off the wing, with D_6 and D_1
adjusting accordingly. As D_1
slides to support D_6, he
leaves X_1 open on the edge
of the crease. D_3 must sink
down to support D_1 (B).

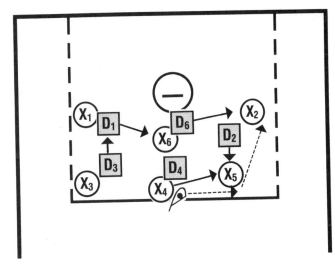

Two Men Down

When forced to play two men down, the defense must stay in tight and give up the outside shot. It's tough for any defensive team to pressure the ball behind the goal when down by two men. Each off-ball defender should sag heavy to the crease and be ready to slide out and play two attackers as long as possible.

Shut Off

Occasionally the MDD can disrupt an extra-man offensive attempt by shutting off one attacker and playing five versus four. The most effective man to shut off is usually the attackman at the point behind the goal. The remaining four defenders should tighten up and set up a zone around the goal area.

CLEARING

After a save, the goalie should look quickly upfield for an outlet pass. If nothing develops, he should go behind the goal and use the crease to kill time off the penalty. By the rules of lacrosse, a team that is down a man cannot be called for stalling. Therefore, the goalie can play cat-and-mouse by running around the crease as long as necessary. The moment the riding team sends a second man to jump the goalie, someone will be open for a pass. Any man-down defender on the perimeter who comes up with a loose ball should be aware of the goalie as a potential release, that is, someone to whom he can potentially pass if he finds himself up against heavy coverage.

MDD-unit awareness of how much time remains in a penalty can assist in the clearing effort and may lead to a fast break. The sixth defender should be sent down from the midline just as the man in the penalty box steps on the offensive side of the field. Alert MDD teams that gain possession just as the penalty expires can pass quickly upfield to this defender as he pops open at the midfield. If the penalty expires and the defense has not gained possession, the sixth defender should sprint to the hole area and call, "All even! Check off!" The defense must then pick up men from the inside out—that is, it must identify and defend the offensive players nearest the crease first, and then pick up the remaining offensive players on the perimeter. They must do this in order to make a clean transition from man-down defense to all even, or six versus six, defense.

Defensive movement when a penalty expires.

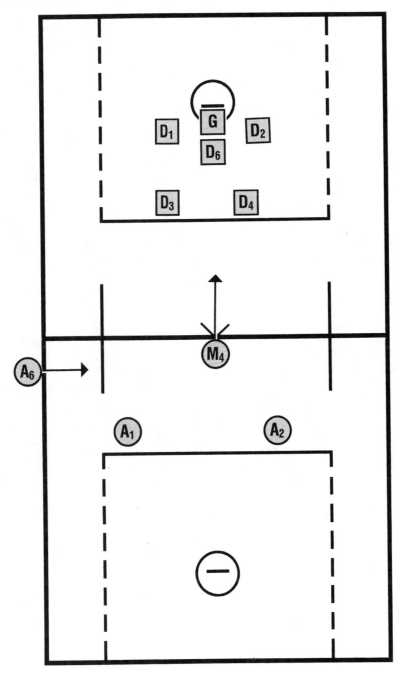

Here we see correct defensive movement when a penalty expires. A_6 steps on the offensive side of the field, releasing M_4 at the midline to hustle in on defense.

Man-down defenders must be extra alert, both when playing off the ball and when moving in to help teammates. Communication and anticipation are key.

Clearing the ball from an out-of-bounds situation allows the man-down team to get a fast, dodging, midfielder into the game. The remaining four defenders should spread out and give the midfielder an opportunity to run the ball over the midline and into the attack goal area. An attempt to jump or double team the run-out middie will leave one man open for a clearing pass. The defender left open must call for the ball and get in position to receive a pass.

Smart lacrosse teams normally have a predetermined "Mayday" spot in the offensive half of the field. In the event the MDD secures possession but is receiving heavy riding pressure, it can execute a long pass to this predetermined spot. A "Mayday" spot is particularly helpful when attempting to clear while a team is two men down.

MAN-DOWN DEFENSIVE MAXIMS

1. Identify the EMO formation and adjust your MDD accordingly.
2. Poke when on the ball, keep your stick up when off the ball.
3. Keep your head on a swivel and call out cutters, that is, when you see someone cut toward the goal, yell "Cutter!"
4. Communicate: Talk and listen.
5. Help on the crease if necessary.
6. Sag heavy to the ball and toward the hole—that is, back in toward the edge of the crease.
7. Anticipate: Be under control.
8. Do not leave the crease early to play a man behind. *Return* to the crease as quickly as possible after playing a man behind the goal.
9. Rotate into the ball from inside out.
10. Do not relax after a man in your area has made a pass. Work hard when off the ball.

9

The Transition Game

Fast breaks (four on three) are perhaps the most exciting plays in lacrosse. Many transition scoring opportunities are initiated by a defensive turnover or a quick outlet pass after a save. It's a pleasure to watch an alert, fast-breaking offense advance the ball quickly the length of the field with great open field speed and precision passes. The defense simultaneously hustles into the hole area to hastily organize a last line of defense. The ultimate challenge unfolds as the offense approaches the goal area with a fast break. Will the breaking team outmaneuver and frustrate the defenders with quick passes that culminate with a net-ripping shot? Or will the defense rise to the occasion and short-circuit the break with great anticipation or a great one-on-one save by the goalie?

Most scoring plays in a lacrosse game occur following a penalty (EMO) or after a quick change of possession. Anytime the offense can advance the ball into the attack goal area with a manpower advantage over the defense, an excellent scoring opportunity should develop.

Transition lacrosse is fun and should be stressed at every practice. Fast breaks (four on three) or slow breaks (five on four, six on five, six on four) may occur at any time: off the face-off, after a save, off the ride, or at the end of a clear. Everyone must be alert to recognize and take full advantage of potential transition scoring opportunities. Let's first examine the transition offense, then concentrate on defending the various break situations.

FAST-BREAK (FOUR-ON-THREE) OFFENSE

From their vantage point in the offense half of the field, the three attackmen should be able to anticipate potential fast breaks. As has been mentioned, a fast break can materialize quickly and unexpectedly. The attack will quite often be

181

Fast breaks can develop at any time. Here we see a break develop following a loose ball on a face-off.

fairly far removed from the goal as the fast break begins to develop. As quickly as possible, and without turning their backs to the ball, the three attackmen must sprint to the hole area and establish their positions. A traditional box or rectangle formation is most often used by the three attackmen and the ballcarrier.

Whenever possible, it's advisable that the attackmen go to predetermined spots on the perimeter of the box. The attack positions for a fast break are referred to as:

1. The point man (A_1)
2. Right-hander's wing (A_2)
3. Left-hander's wing (A_3)

Each spot requires special skills. It's not always possible for the attack to assume their predetermined positions; therefore they must be comfortable at any of the three spots.

Let's examine the fast break from the standpoint of each of the four offensive players involved in the four on three.

The Ballcarrier (M_4)

Usually, one of the three midfielders will bring the ball down on a four on three. It's not unusual, however, for a defenseman to fill this spot. The ballcarrier must sprint toward the goal area, making sure he is slightly favoring one side of the field. He should carry his stick to the outside (sideline) and focus his attention on the defensive triangle.

The primary responsibility of the break man (M_4) is to drive hard enough at the goal to draw defensive pressure from the point defenseman (D_1). A well-drilled defense will stay in tight. Therefore, M_4 may have to penetrate well inside the restraining line before the defense reacts.

If no one attempts to stop M_4, he will continue to the goal and shoot. If the point defenseman (D_1) slides over to stop the ball, M_4 must now read the situation. Most of the time M_4 will execute a crisp pass to the point attackman (A_1). However, if he reads D_2 making a premature rotation, M_4 can make a diagonal pass to A_2 for a close-range shot. If he reads D_3 making an early rotation across the goal, M_4 can pass down the side to A_3 for a shot.

M_4's primary responsibility is to draw a man toward himself and to look to pass to the appropriate attackman. Faking a pass to A_1 will often open up a direct pass to A_2 for an easy close shot. After releasing the ball, M_4 will look for a possible return pass, or cut to the goal for a feed in the hole area.

Point Attackman (A₁)

The point man is the quarterback. He must be able to read the defense and make crisp, accurate passes on a split-second's notice. A_1 establishes a position just inside the restraining line and on the opposite side of the field as the breaking middie (M_4). If the point man reads that the middie is approaching from the right side of the field, he must pull to the left. The point man should start out wide and move toward the middle of the field with his stick to the outside. Let's examine a fast break with the midfielder (M_4) approaching from the right side of the field.

A traditional 4 versus 3 fast break.

In a traditional 4 versus 3 fast break, the offense's motto should be "Let the ball do the work." Crisp passes to the edge of the box area are critical. M_4 must make the defense react, then pass diagonally to either A_2 or the point man, A_1 (A).

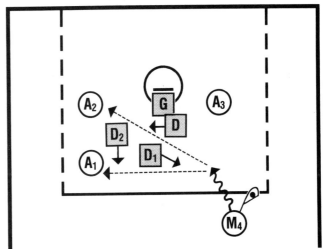

The point man, A_1, is a key figure in the fast break offense. If he receives a pass from M_4, he can pass to A_2, A_3, or M_4, or move in and shoot, depending on how the defense reacts (B).

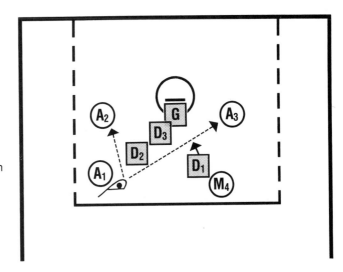

If D_1 slides prematurely, M_4 will pass to A_1 early. If M_4 continues toward the goal uncontested, the point man (A_1) must move with him, staying in his line of vision. Once the point defenseman (D_1) commits to M_4, A_1 will receive the ball and has the following options:

1. He can pass down the side to A_2.
2. He can look at an angle to A_3 for a left-handed shot.
3. If uncontested, he can move in and shoot.
4. He can give a return pass to M_4.
5. He can take a check from D_2 and then look to pass or shoot.

To make these quick decisions, A_1 must receive plenty of practice. He should always receive the ball to the outside, near his ear. Presenting a good target is essential. Likewise, A_1's passes must also be to the outside "box" area. Nothing will short-circuit a fast break more quickly than passes to the inside. A_1 can really open up his options on the fast break by faking passes and drawing the defense out of position.

Right-Handed Wing (A_2)

This is the right-handed shooter's spot. A_2 must be a finisher, able to withstand a check and still shoot. A_2 will sprint back to the GLE, four to six yards off the edge of the crease. That is only a starting point. As the ball is thrown to A_2, he will move hard to meet the pass and to increase his shooting angle. He must concentrate on getting his shoulders turned toward the goal before he shoots. A_2 should be alert for a diagonal pass from M_4 or a direct pass from the point man (A_1). A_2's options are:

1. Shoot, looking to the far side of the goal or between the goalie and the near pipe.
2. Pass across the plane of the goal to A_3, if D_3 has made a good slide.
3. Pass to M_4 or A_1 moving into the hole.
4. Take a check from an over-aggressive D_3 sliding across the goal. This will place you right in front of the goal.

It's critical that A_2 anticipate a shot from either M_4, A_1, or A_3. He must be ready to race to the endline so the offense will retain possession if the shot travels out of bounds.

Left-Handed Wing (A$_3$)

A$_3$ will assume the same relative position as A$_2$ on the left side of the goal. He is primarily a shooter and should have a strong left hand. A$_3$ must be able to finish the classic fast-break sequence: midfielder (M$_4$) to point man (A$_1$) to right-hander (A$_2$) to left-hander (A$_3$). A$_3$ may find the goalie way out of position. A perfect shot is not always necessary, and it's important not to baby your shot from here. Be sure to shoot it hard. Really stick it.

A$_3$ has the same basic options as A$_2$. He also has the responsibility of backing up the goal on shots by M$_4$, A$_1$, and A$_2$.

SLOW BREAKS (FIVE ON FOUR, SIX ON FIVE, SIX ON FOUR)

There are many transition situations in a lacrosse game other than a pure four-on-three, when the offense has a definite numbers advantage over the defense. The term slow break is often used to describe a six on five, five on four, or six on four offensive advantage. It is obviously much easier to score a transition goal than a six on six goal. Everyone, therefore, should be alert to recognize and to take full advantage of slow-break opportunities.

Teams that make effective use of the sideline and are corner conscious when clearing the ball will enjoy plenty of slow-break opportunities. As the ball starts to move out of the defensive half of the field, the two wing attackmen (A$_1$ and A$_2$) should position themselves outside the goal area and slightly above the GLE. Teammates who are experiencing riding pressure between the restraining lines must be able to depend on these two releases in the corners. Passing the ball to either wing attackman in the corners not only facilitates the clear, but may also catch the defense far enough upfield to give the offense a slow break.

As the ball is passed to a wing attackman in the corner, the opposite wing will cut to the point behind the goal. The attackman with the ball should make the pass from the GLE. This serves to prevent the goalie from intercepting the pass. The wing attackman moving to the point should run along the GLE, fake a "front swing," across the mouth of the goal, and then break to the point behind the goal.

While the ball is being passed down the sideline and to the point behind, the midfielders must hustle towards the goal area to enter into a cutting pattern with the crease attackman. The timing of the cuts to the goal is very important. The attackman at the point should have control of the ball and be in a good position to feed before anyone cuts.

A typical "slow break."

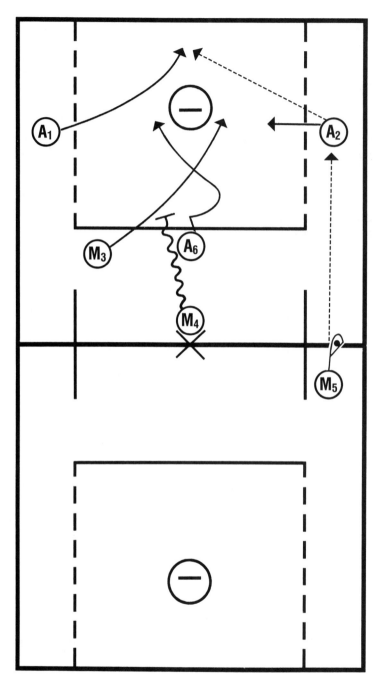

In this slow break situation, M_5 dumps the ball to A_2 in the corner. A_1 receives the ball at the point behind and immediately looks to the crease for a possible feed (A).

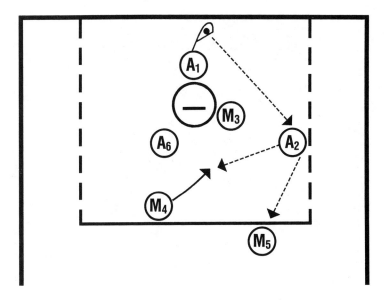

If A_1 elects not to feed either cutter, he can quickly redirect the ball back to A_2, who is positioned just above the GLE on the corner. A_2 now has a few options: 1) He can feed a trailing midfielder (M_4). 2) He can pass up top to M_5. 3) He can move toward the goal, draw a defender toward himself, and look to feed M_3 on the crease, or A_1 on a sneak. If M_5 receives a return pass, he can drive and shoot from outside or look to feed the weak side (B).

The crease attackman ($\overline{A_6}$) will cut for himself, trying to catch the defenders with their backs turned. He will normally make a hard, direct cut at one of the goal pipes. The first midfielder down the field will read this move and cut down the opposite pipe. The attackman at the point will look to feed either cutter. If he elects not to make a feed, the point attackman then redirects the ball immediately back to the wing attackman who passed it to him. The ball is then passed up top to a trailing midfielder for a possible outside shot (with screens) or a quick dodge and shot.

The keys to a successful slow break are quick ball movement, accurate passes, and well-timed cuts. If you are open, the ball will find you. Cut when you have a clear path to the goal. Do not drag a defender into the hole area where he may be able to defend more than one cutter.

Slow Breaks

The key to a successful slow break (5 versus 4, 6 versus 5, 6 versus 4) is letting the ball do the work. Here, #4, in the left foreground, looks for a pass or a shot.

Containing a pure four-on-three fast break presents the defense with a real challenge. The three close defensemen must stay in tight, anticipate, and use well-coordinated zone principles to cover the prime shooting areas and take away the high percentage shots.

The moment a fast break develops upfield, the goalie takes control of the defense and urges it to retreat to the hole area. The close defense must sprint to the hole, always keeping the ball in sight. The three defenders form a tight triangle, with the point defenseman (D_1) aligning 10 to 12 yards in front of the goal. Since the three defenders are likely to be sprinting to the hole area from various spots upfield, communication is essential. The point defenseman (D_1) must make it clear, "I've got the point," so the two remaining defenders can adjust accordingly. "Back right" (D_2) and "Back left" (D_3) calls by the respective defenders will ensure that all three defenders are in proper position. It's wise not to assume too much. Talk is the key.

Let's examine the movements and responsibilities of each of the three defenders. To facilitate the explanation, we'll analyze a fast break with the midfielder (M_4) approaching from the defensive left side of the field, and the point attackman (A_1) setting up to the defensive right.

Point Defenseman (D_1)

The defenseman closest to the ball or in the middle portion of the field will normally identify himself as the "point" man. Where the point man establishes his position in the triangle is crucial. He must sprint to a point 10 yards in front of the goal, assume a balanced, square position, and prepare to meet the advancing midfielder (M_4). He and the other defenders are covering zones; therefore eye contact with the ball and good vertical stick position become paramount for all three defenders.

As the ball approaches, D_1 moves out under control and tries to check M_4's stick or block any passing attempts. D_1 must stop M_4 physically, though mentally he is anticipating a pass and his own corresponding reaction. D_1 cannot afford to rush out at M_4, nor should he move more than 12 yards from the goal.

As the break man (M_4) makes a pass, the point man (D_1) pivots, with his eyes fixed on the ball, and hustles to the crease area. D_1 should keep his stick up to discourage, or to knock down, any diagonal passes attempted through the hole area. The point defenseman's job really begins *after* M_4 has made a pass. He must be alert to pivot *with the ball in sight* and to hustle toward the crease. *Do not* turn your back to the ball.

The fast-break defense.

Notice the tight triangle alignment of the fast-break defense. D_1 pivots, always keeping the ball in sight after he forces M_4 to throw a pass. D_2 and D_3 slide in toward the ball. Anticipation and discipline are keys for the defense (A).

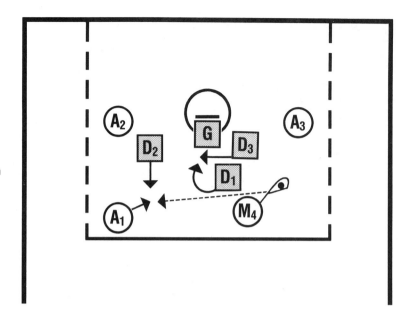

As D_1 slides toward the hole, D_2 rotates up to challenge A_1, and D_3 anticipates the next pass. Each player tunes in to the goalie for directions, and everyone communicates as a unit (B).

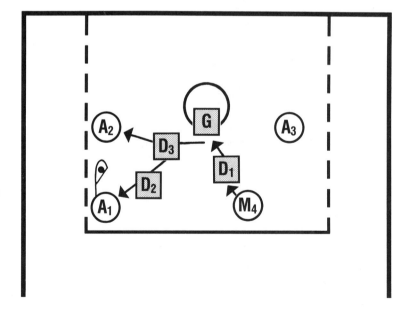

Back Right Defenseman (D$_2$)

D$_2$ aligns just outside the right goal post and a few yards in front of the front edge of the crease. His stick is up as he splits (divides his coverage between) A$_1$ and A$_2$, attempting to read where M$_4$ will pass the ball. If M$_4$ passes to the point attackman (A$_1$), D$_2$ must slide out to challenge him with a poke check. D$_2$ must be careful not to rotate up too quickly, opening up A$_2$ on the edge of the crease for a direct pass from M$_4$.

After sliding out under control to challenge A$_1$ on the point, D$_2$ must be ready to react to the path of the next pass. A return pass back to M$_4$ or a diagonal pass to A$_3$ will mean D$_2$ must open to the inside and sprint back to the hole, keeping his stick up and eyes on the ball. If A$_1$ passes down the side to A$_2$, D$_2$ must pivot to the outside with his eyes on the ball and drop inside.

Back Left Defenseman (D$_3$)

D$_3$ assumes the same relative position as D$_2$, but a little closer to the middle of the goal. D$_3$ is responsible for A$_3$, but he must anticipate and be ready to slide across the front of the crease to challenge A$_2$. If D$_3$ leaves too early to check A$_2$, A$_3$ will be open for a diagonal pass from the point attackman (A$_1$).

It's important to understand that the reaction and movement of the defenders occurs simultaneously. They must practice constantly to be able to think alike and anticipate each other's movements.

The defensive midfielder who is trailing the play must sprint to the hole to assist in whatever way possible. He should alert his teammates that it is "all even" or that there is "no break." The three close defensemen should react by calling out the jersey numbers of their respective attackmen and pick them up from the inside out. It's not unusual following a fast break for the defense to play different men than they were originally.

FAST-BREAK DEFENSIVE MAXIMS

1. Sprint to the hole, keeping the ball in sight.
2. Form a tight triangle with sticks up to the inside.
3. Communicate and anticipate.
4. Do not rush at people. Break downfield with good body position and poke.
5. Do not turn your back to the ball. Pivot with it, keeping it always in sight.
6. Call out numbers and pick up inside out when it is all even.
7. Do whatever it takes to get in that last-moment check.

FAST-BREAK DEFENSIVE DRILLS

There are two excellent progression drills that reinforce fast-break defensive principles:

Triangle to the Ball

Two defenders work in tandem surrounded by three offensive players aligned in a triangle. The defender on the ball will break down and poke after clearly stating "I've got the ball." As a pass is made to either adjacent point of the triangle, the defender who was on the ball pivots with the pass and moves to position, splitting the two remaining attackers.

The off-ball defender moves into position to challenge the ballcarrier with a poke check and a "Ball" call. As the ball is passed around the triangle, the two defenders pivot and slide accordingly.

The Triangle-to-the-Ball Drill

This drill reinforces sound defensive fundamentals. The two defenders inside the triangle work to maintain their original tandem position. One defender challenges the ballcarrier while the other splits his coverage of the two remaining offensive players. Both defenders should always pivot to keep the ball in sight.

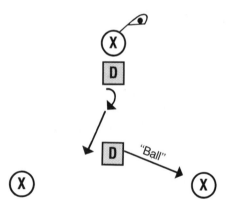

Rectangle to the Ball

This takes the triangle drill one step further. Three defenders work together inside four perimeter passers aligned in a rectangle. The defense works to maintain a triangle relationship with the ball. One man plays the "ball," one defender is "back right," and one is "back left." The defenders keep their sticks up to the inside to discourage diagonal passes. As the ball moves around the outside of the rectangle, all three defenders must pivot and slide accordingly. If a diagonal pass does get through, the two off-ball defenders must communicate and decide which one will take the ball and which one will be a backup. The players on the perimeter of the rectangle should not rush their passes. Give the defense a second or two to react.

The Rectangle-to-the-Ball Drill

This drill challenges the three inside defenders to maintain their original tight triangle alignment as they try to break up the offensive players' passes and force a turnover. Sticks are up and to the inside to deny the diagonal pass. Communication and anticipation are required as the ball is passed around the rectangle.

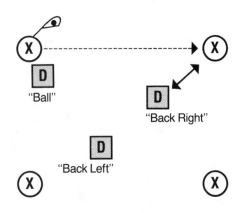

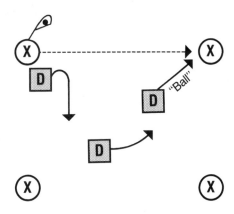

Fast-Break Defense

A

Fast-break defense places strong emphasis on staying tight, playing under control, and making maximum use of stick length. Notice here how the defender simultaneously poke-checks and pivots, keeping his eyes fixed on the ball.

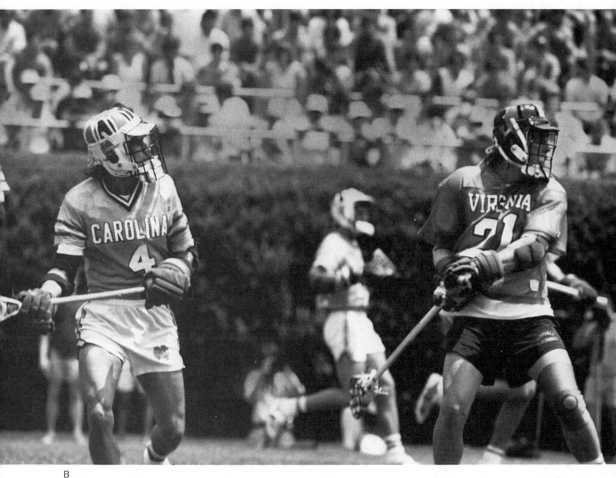

B

Proper emphasis and time spent on the transition game is a must for all lacrosse teams. Teams must be drilled to recognize and take full advantage of any situation that presents them with a numerical offensive advantage. Conversely, transition defense must be stressed and drilled everyday in practice.

10

Goalie Play

The goalkeeper is obviously a team's last line of defense. He must save the ball, quarterback the team defense, and provide the intangible cohesive qualities of a winner. All great teams have strong goaltenders who extend themselves beyond the immediate task of stopping the ball.

As in goalie play in soccer and hockey, body position and attention to playing the angles are very important. Defending the 6-ft by 6-ft lacrosse goal against low skimming shots, various types of bounce shots, and high hard shots presents the lacrosse goalie with a real challenge.

PRIVILEGES AND PROTECTIONS

Within his goal-crease area, the goalkeeper may stop or block the ball in any manner, with his stick or his body. He may block the ball or bat it away with his hand, but he may not catch the ball with his hand. The goalie or any member of the defending team may receive a pass while in the crease area; however, they may remain within the goal crease in possession of the ball no longer than four seconds.

No opposing player may make contact with the goalkeeper or his stick while he and the ball are within the goal-crease area, whether he has the ball in his possession or not. As an attacking player, you may reach within the crease area to play a loose ball, so long as you do not make contact with the goalkeeper or his stick. An attacking player may not be in the opponent's goal-crease area at any time while the ball is in the offensive half of the field. A defending player, including the goalkeeper, with the ball in his possession, outside the crease may not reenter the crease. Reentry while in possession of the ball results in a technical foul and loss of possession.

197

The goalkeeper is the heart and soul of a lacrosse team. He should be a strong leader and a good athlete.

The goalkeeper has the potential to be the most dominating player in the game, yet many times he is the least coached. Many coaches realize that goalie is a position that requires a good athlete, but are unable to help channel the athlete's energy in the proper areas. I will try to explain not only the proper techniques in good goaltending, but also how to teach them.

EQUIPMENT

It is extremely important for goaltenders to be fully protected at all times. If you're a goalie, you must learn to accept that getting hit with the ball from time to time is inevitable. There are a few pieces of equipment designed for you, to help take the sting out of shots which strike the body.

The throat guard or bib has recently become mandatory at the secondary and collegiate levels. The throat guard is a foam pad attached to the lower portion of the face mask, extending down and offering protection to the throat area. A chest protector worn under the jersey is also a required piece of goalie equipment. Many goalies also choose to wear a pair of warm-up pants or sweatpants to help take the sting out of shots which strike their legs. This is a matter of individual preference, and is not required. Gloves are also required, and I recommend that any goalie wear a protective cup.

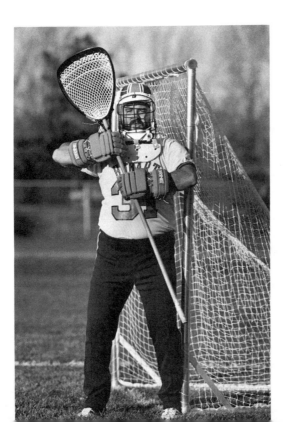

Goalie Equipment

Stick, gloves, helmet, mask, and throat bib are all mandatory equipment for the goalkeeper. A long-sleeved jersey and sweatpants, while not mandatory, do provide added protection.

The goalie stick is distinctly different from the sticks used by players at other positions. The head of the goalie's stick is considerably wider than attack, midfield, or defense sticks, and there is no restriction on the depth of the pocket. The increased surface area allows the goalie to protect the goal more efficiently, and a deep, sagging pocket helps the goalie control hard shots without the ball rebounding out of his stick.

The wide head and deep pocket of the goalie's stick require a different passing technique. The deep, sagging pocket allows the goalie to protect the ball, and facilitates dodging. The width of the stick, however, allows more ball movement, making it harder to control the ball. Accurate passing with a goalie's stick requires much more wrist motion than is necessary with attack, midfield, or defense sticks. Before you attempt a pass, you should stabilize the ball as much as possible in the pocket of the stick with a sweeping, cradling motion. In order to ensure the proper wrist motion, you should extend the stick well back, and use a catapult type motion to release the ball.

MENTAL AND PHYSICAL REQUIREMENTS

The good goaltender possesses a combination of traits that come together to make him effective. These traits range from hand and foot speed to leadership ability. For a coach, one of the more difficult chores is to discern which traits are more desirable than others to the team as a whole.

The following is a list of traits which are necessary to a good goaltender. There are eight aspects to goalie play which can be divided into two categories: the mental and the physical. These traits are all closely related, as are the two categories.

Mental: Concentration
Leadership
Confidence
Knowledge of the game

Physical: Quickness (hands and feet)
Clearing ability
Positioning
Stopping ability

Concentration

Lacrosse goalies face the double challenge of stopping the ball and directing the team defense. Total concentration is the key.

Concentration

This is the one trait which is necessary to every good goalkeeper. Many times even super athletic ability cannot overcome lack of concentration. If you're a goalie, it's essential that you always concentrate on the ball. This means the ball, and not the stick. Further, you must always concentrate on the *present* and *never* the past. A goal scored should become a goal forgotten. If you concentrate well, you'll better maintain your position, see the ball more clearly, and direct your defense more efficiently. Most important, if you concentrate well, you'll be able to be the most technique-conscious.

Leadership

To be a good leader as a goalie, you must be poised, confident, and enthusiastic. The goaltender is very visible to the whole team, and that gives him the opportunity to bring them together. To be a leader, you must earn respect. The best way to do this is to show your teammates you will do anything to stop the ball. The good goalie is also a good talker. To be effective, the talk must be selective and timely. Ball location with respect to the goal, "Check" calls on all feeds, and "Break" or "Clear" calls must be part of your narrative. The real challenge for a goalie is to talk and lead effectively with his voice, but not at the expense of his concentration.

Try to be a leader by bringing the defense together after a goal or before a man-down situation. When making voice commands, be firm and use inflections. Good goalies must be both encouraging *and* demanding.

Confidence

This is another one of the critical mental aspects. You should have the type of confidence that borders on cockiness. Coaches, confidence is something that you can and must instill in your goalie. This can be achieved through proper warmup practices and the monitoring of the shots the goalie faces in practice. Never yell at a goalkeeper after a goal is scored. Always approach him calmly and explain what he could have done to have a better chance at the ball. The more confidence a goalkeeper has in himself, the more confidence the team will have in him.

Knowledge of the Game

This includes not only the knowledge of the proper techniques of his position, but also offensive strategies, clearing and riding philosophies, and the ability to recognize what an opponent is attempting to accomplish. The goalie should function as a computer on the field, taking in all available information and making quick decisions. One of the best ways to bring your goalie to this level is by talking with him one-on-one. First determine what he knows and try to help him from that point. You may also want to present him with hypothetical situations and ask for his reaction. It is also helpful to practice staged situations.

Quickness

This is a physical trait which should not be confused with speed. As a goalie, you can get by with only marginal foot quickness but hand quickness is essential. There are many ways to increase both foot *and* hand quickness. The best way to work on both is to jump rope. If hand quickness needs to be improved, an effective practice is to play with a heavy or weighted stick. The faster you are, the more effective you can be in disrupting the offense in the goal area. Good foot quickness better allows you to intercept passes to and from the point behind, and to come out and hit an attackman coming around the cage.

Clearing Ability

The lacrosse goalie takes a much more active role in clearing the ball than his counterpart in either hockey or soccer. Lacrosse goalies must be able to handle the ball comfortably upfield, away from the goal. In addition to making quick outlet passes to teammates breaking upfield after a save, lacrosse goalies must also coordinate settled clearing attempts which require several passes in the defensive half of the field.

Many teams, especially at the high school level, clear the ball without making proper use of their goaltender. Many times this is not by choice, but due to the coach's lack of confidence in the goalie's clearing ability. Good stickhandling is an obvious necessity. As a goalie, you should be one of the best on the team at handling a stick. It can be beneficial, especially if you're a younger player, to use an attack stick to play catch in your free time. The sooner you master this stick, the easier it will be for you to handle the big stick. The ability to throw the quick outlet pass is invaluable, and you should practice this skill. This can be done during a warmup or by setting time aside before and after practice. In order for such work to be qualitative, the man catching your passes should be moving at full speed. Good judgment is also a key to smart clearing. You must know when to push it up the field and when to slow it down. The first look should always be to where the shot came from. Against a soft ride, the goalie should be patient and be ready to look deep. It's also helpful if coaches can teach their goalie to be the eyes of other players when he, the goalie, does not have the ball.

A

B

Positioning: Ball Out Front

Goalies must become comfortable working along an imaginary arc in front of the plane of the goal (A). As the ball sweeps across the field, the goalie moves with it along his arc (B,C,D).

POSITIONING

This concern encompasses many of the others, but has been singled out because of the importance it holds in good goaltending. To maintain the proper position, you must be relaxed yet keep an aggressive frame of mind. One of the keys to good position is proper balance—again, something you can improve via rope jumping and weight training. One of the first things you must master is the position of your body on the "arc." The "arc" is an imaginary line that forms a semicircle and connects the two pipes. This imaginary line should always run concurrent with the crease. Some goalies have an arc that is close to the goal mouth; others tend to play farther away. Each individual goalie must find his own arc, although he should be aware of the consequences if his arc is too small or too large. When finding your arc, you should avoid the two extremes. Playing too close will give up too much angle and make it more difficult for you against teams that pass well. If you play too far away from the goal mouth, you will be plagued by the same problems. Many goalies find it useful to make reference marks to help them maintain good position. It's also important to be aware of the field conditions. That will help you to determine what type of bounce you will be facing. When the ball is in front of the cage, you should keep your body in direct line between the ball and the middle of the net. Be prepared to make adjustments if the shooter switches hands.

C

D

Ball Behind

When the ball is behind the net, you must be as careful about your position as you are when the ball is in front. The method of defense you choose can be based solely on personal preference, but one thing that must remain constant is the position of your stick. Always try to keep your lower hand at the bottom of your stick and your top hand in the middle. The stick should be kept straight up and down and moved in a telescopic fashion. To help deny feeds over the top of the goal, let the stick slide through your top hand and anticipate feeding situations.

The three methods you can use when the ball is behind goal are:

1. *Stay in the middle.* Remain stationary at the top of your arc, only turning your body to face the ball.

2. *Mirror the ball.* Here, you stay on the same side of the goal that the ball is on. Your position should remain flatter to the goal than in the other two methods.

3. *Opposite the ball.* Here, you work on the same arc you move on when the ball is out front. Try always to form a straight line through the middle of the cage between your body and the ball. I believe every goalie should play this way when down a man, as it helps to take away back door feeds (passes from behind the goal, or near the GLE, or diagonally across the back of the cage to the far side of the goal).

STOPPING THE BALL

Stance

To get a quick jump on the ball, an efficient, comfortable stance is essential. Your feet should be shoulders' width apart. If your feet are too wide apart, they can limit your mobility; if they are too close together, they can cause you to be off balance. The weight of your body should be kept on the balls of your feet. It's also a good idea to to stand slightly pigeon-toed. This will help you keep your weight on the *insides* of your feet, from which you can push to get to the ball. Along the same lines, it's advantageous if you can stand slightly knock-kneed. To be as efficient as possible, always keep your back straight. A straight back will help you maintain good foot position and balance, which will help on rebounds. Keep your shoulders back, but not too much, and your head stationary and erect.

Positioning: Ball Behind the Goal

The goalie has three positioning options when the ball is behind the goal. He can stay in the middle of the goal (A), he can mirror the ball (B), or he can position himself opposite the ball (C) to discourage back-door feeds.

A

B

C

Stance

Proper stance (A).

Hands

This aspect of goalie play is one of the most important. Technique flaws in this area will result in goals. Your top hand should be at, or near, the throat of the stick. Your bottom hand should be 8 to 12 inches down from the top hand. These hand positions should always be maintained and never compromised, as the wrong technique can be very costly. A reliable indicator that your hands are too far apart is when you find that reaching the off-hip shot is difficult. If your hands are too close together, there will be a noticeable lack of control in the movement of the stick. A key phrase to good goalie play is "Lead with the hands." Many of the top-level goalies will make as many as 90 percent of their saves with the stick. If a goalie is leading with his hands, this momentum will take his body right to the ball. Leading with the hands is perhaps the most important mechanical factor in stopping the ball.

You should also learn to keep your hands *away from your body*. Coaches, a good practice is to tell your goalkeeper to keep his hands in front of him at all times. This should also hold true for his elbows. Many goalies make the mistake of keeping their elbows too close to their body. The elbows should be relaxed and away from the body, but not so far that the position feels awkward or uncomfortable.

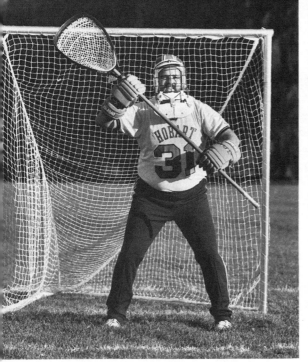

Hands and feet both too far apart (B).

Hands and feet both too close together (C).

Step

Stepping properly is one technique that good goalies realize is essential to stopping the ball. Playing goal, you should visualize yourself split right down the middle. On any shot to your right side, you should step with your right foot; on any shot to your left side, you should step with your left foot. The step should always be taken at a good angle to the ball, and you should try to end in the same stance in which you started. The idea is to have the ball hit you dead center (split you down the middle) after you have finished your move. After completing the step, your feet should still be about shoulder width apart. This holds true for both low and high shots. Remember also to bring your trail foot in the step and not to drag it. After making the step, your feet should be pointing out—a position that adds extra saving surface and could help block shots, especially those taken in tight. Always lift the foot comfortably. Don't shuffle, hop, or stride.

Stick Position

Many coaches advocate lowering the goalie's stick as the shooter's distance from the goal increases. I believe that the stick should always be kept high—especially against top-level competition. As players become better shooters, they can shoot high from anywhere on the field, and if a goalie is holding his stick low it calls for an unnatural upward movement to make the save. If the shot is taken from out front and is low, the goalie will still have time to react, since the downward movement he will make is more natural. The grip on the stick should be firm, but the arms must stay relaxed. The stick should be held right next to the head to deny greater shooting space.

TYPES OF SHOTS

High Shots

What's the best way to stop high shots? You should play them as if you were playing catch. You should also be encouraged to try to get your body *behind* the shot, though that is sometimes more difficult to do than on a low shot. Concentration is very important because you must see the ball clearly. Your hands play a critical role on a high shot, as the ball is less likely to hit your body than on a low shot.

Shots From in Tight

The key to playing this type of shot is to *keep your stick on the same level as the ball.* If an opponent is carrying the ball high, your stick should be on the same plane. The same holds true if the ball is being held on any other plane. Anticipation is a must in this situation as sometimes quickness is just not enough. The saves you make in tight deserve the most praise even if the shooter appears to have merely hit you with a shot, since actually the save could have been a matter of your good positioning. On such "stuff saves," you should come up into the ball but never quite extend your arms completely. If you extend your arms all the way, reacting to rebounds will be difficult. Always remember that any time a shooter is in tight he should score, so a shot wide or off the pipe is as good as a save. Coaches, when your team is practicing these shots, it does not hurt morale to make sure your keeper saves a few.

Shots From a Feed

Keeping the ball clearly and constantly in sight when it is being fed from one player to another for a possible shot is an absolute must, since the ball can cover up to 30 yards in a matter of seconds and the shot itself might come the moment

The High-Shot Save

Notice how the goalie steps at the ball (A), leads with his hands (B), and completes the save with a cradle at the edge of the crease (C).

A

B

C

the shooter receives the feed. Following the flight of the ball from a feeder behind the goal to a shooter in front of the goal presents the goalie with perhaps his toughest challenge. He must pivot or turn as the pass is made, then refocus and position himself to make an instantaneous save.

When following the flight of the ball on a feed from behind the goal, try to make a 180-degree turn with your stick up, and be prepared to stop the shot instantly. As you make the turn toward the front, you should be moving *toward the ball.* A common error is to turn in place. Too, you must maintain a fine balance between aggressiveness and relaxation. To successfully defend against shots on feed, you must pull out all the stops and do anything you can to stop the ball. A loud clear "Check" call will alert the team defense that a feed has been made and to check sticks. Alert goalies constantly try to block or intercept any feeds from behind that travel over, or near, the goal. It's important as a goalie to deny any feeds over the goal. However, don't be preoccupied with blocking passes at the expense of not being in proper position, or not making an effective turn and subsequent save.

Low Shots

Low shots demand the most technique from the goalie—everything must come together in order for him to consistently stop the low shot. The proper technique will afford him an efficiency of movement which will prove invaluable. In general, as a goalie, never sweep at a low shot. Nor should your stick sweep past the ball. Instead, take your stick directly to the ball in the most efficient manner and keep it there. After completing that move, return your stick to its original position in front of you. The stick should not be so far from your feet as to cause overextension, but it should not be right at your feet either. A good way to determine that your stick is in the proper position is by the position of your elbows. If they are in tight to your body, chances are the stick is in too close. During a save on a low shot, your step should be straight to the ball and not at the man or the stick. The best way to improve this aspect of your game is by repetition. Coaches, a quantity of shots taken at less than full speed can help your goalie tremendously if the goalie's technique is closely observed and corrected, as necessary.

Playing the Feed

Turning to make a save off a
feed is perhaps the most
difficult technique for a goalie to
master. Here, the goalie pivots
with the ball, keeping his stick
up and the ball in sight (A,B). At
the moment of the feed, the
goalie steps out away from the
goal in anticipation of the
probable shot (C,D).

A

B

C

D

A   B

The Low-Shot Save

On bounce shots, the rule is "Step at the ball." Here the goalkeeper steps (A) and makes the save (B), his momentum carrying his right foot outside the crease.

COMMUNICATION

As the leader of the defense, you must constantly communicate with your teammates. The more constructive narrative you can provide without sacrificing your own concentration, the better everyone on defense will ultimately

Playing the Screen

When confronted with a screen, the goalie works on a higher arc (A), and bends at the waist (B) to try to improve his sight-line. To make the save, he steps in the direction of the shot (C,D).

A   B

perform. Location of the ball with respect to the goal ("Front right," "Front center," "Back left," and so on) should be continuously vocalized to alert all the defenders. Encouraging your defense to "poke," slide," "check," and "hold" will benefit the entire team defensive effort. As an attackman drives around the goal from behind, you can assist the defense by signaling when the attacker is "even" with the plane of the goal. After securing possession of the ball, shout "Break" in a loud voice to signal your team to break upfield, initiating the clear.

PLAYING THE SCREEN

Every good goalie will face a screen at some point in every game. Concentration combined with educated guessing can make playing the screened shot easier. Communication with the defense becomes imperative since they can be told to subtly move the screen out of the way. If the screen remains, you should be thinking low shot, as this is what shooters are taught to take when they have a screen. Furthermore, once the screen has been established, you must react by working on a higher arc—that is, farther out from the plane of the goal. This will allow you a better opportunity to see around or over the screen. If you do try to look around or over a screen, you must always be aware of what you are giving away by doing so. Compensation in this situation can be made by keeping your stick in a different position. At the very least, you should try to see the ball being released so that you can make an educated guess as to where it is going, and can step and get your stick there.

C

D

CLEARING THE BALL

Although the goalie's primary responsibility is to stop the ball, you can help yourself and your team considerably by becoming a proficient clearer. Clearing is the term used to describe the movement of the ball from a team's defensive half of the field into its attack goal area. Goalies can make life less frustrating and significantly advance their own and their team's cause by developing a few basic skills needed to clear the ball consistently.

The rules provide maximum protection for the goalkeeper whenever he has possession of the ball inside the crease. After securing control of the ball while inside the crease, the goalkeeper has four seconds either to make a pass or step out of the circle. As long as the goalie has one foot inside the circle, he is considered in the crease and his stick cannot be checked. Alert goalies can extend one foot outside the crease to clamp and scoop loose balls anywhere near the goal area.

Many goalies do not take full advantage of the four-second rule. Inexperienced goalies tend to rush their clearing passes or run behind the goal immediately after making a save, eliminating any chance for a transition scoring opportunity. The key is to *relax* after making a save, *take a good look*

Clearing

When making an outlet clearing pass, take full advantage of the four-second rule, scan the whole field, and be sure to lead your receiver.

A

upfield, and execute a *smooth clearing pass.* Exiting out the side or back door should be your last option as a goalie. It's a good idea, instead, to look in the direction from which the shot came.

To ensure consistent clearing, you should periodically incorporate breakaway type passes in your warmup. Practice making outlet passes to teammates breaking upfield and over the restraining line. Try not to throw them on a line, but with a slight loft or arc to prevent being intercepted by the riders. The landing zone for these passes should be on the defensive side of the midline— clearing passes that carry over the midline may put the receiver in jeopardy. Be sure to vary the direction of your passes. An alert goalie can initiate transition offense that ultimately may lead to a goal 80 yards down the field.

GOALIE DRILLS

The techniques and skills necessary to become an effective goalie are unique, and thus should be treated as such by coaches. If you're a coach, you should supervise your goalie's drills closely, and constantly emphasize correct technique. If possible, videotape your goalie performing the various drills, allow

B C

him to view himself, and share with him your thoughts and comments about his technique.

The following goalie drills provide an excellent preseason fundamental foundation and can be practiced indoors as well as out. Once the season begins, it's hard to provide your goalie with any more than a thorough warmup. I can say from firsthand experience that time invested with your goalie early in the year will pay healthy dividends as the season progresses.

Down the Line, or Walk the Line

Start in the ready stance, straddling a line. Now imagine a shot coming toward you—low, high, stickside, or off stickside—and react accordingly. This drill is not designed for quickness, but for technique. Do the moves slowly the first few times and exaggerate them to stress technique. If you're a coach, this drill presents a great opportunity to analyze your goalie's technique, from stance and hand position, to the angle of his step. During this drill, you must stress that

The Down-the-Line Drill

In this sequence, the goalie practices his high stick saves (C,B,A), and his low stick saves (C,D,E). In both saves, note the coordinated movement of the stick and body. Note, too, that the stick shaft points directly down after a high stick save, and directly up after a low stick save.

A

B

the goalie should always finish in the same stance in which he started. Always emphasize that he should take his time, especially between shots, making sure he resets himself completely. This drill can be utilized by goalies *before* they begin their warmup in the goal.

Turns on the Wall

This drill simulates a feed from behind and a subsequent quick shot. If you're a goalie, face a wall as if it were the face of the goal, and position yourself approximately two feet from the wall with your stick up. Have your coach then throw the ball high off the wall and prepare to shoot at the goal when the ball rebounds. You should turn when you see the ball hit the wall. This is an exceptional opportunity for the coach to see if you are coming *out* on your turns, that is, moving forward. The coach should also be checking to make sure you are covering the shooter's stick and not his body. Most shots in this drill should be directed towards the top of the goal.

C   D   E

**Over-the-Shoulder,
On-the-Wall**

Once again, face a wall with your coach behind you. This time you should be about 10 to 15 yards from the wall. The coach bounces the ball off the wall and you should play it like a shot. This is another opportunity for the coach to monitor your technique. You can control the reaction time required by how close or far you stand to the wall. This can be good for your quickness if, at the end of the drill, you move about two to three yards from the wall and then try to do anything you can to stop the ball. By altering the angle at which he shoots the ball, your coach can simulate all types of shots for you—high or low, stickside or off stickside.

Loose Ball on the Crease

Stand in the crease while the ball is placed a few yards from the crease. Now rake the ball back into the crease, gain possession, and try to hold it as close to four seconds as possible before throwing an outlet pass. Your coach should use a stopwatch to time you. You may be surprised as to how long four seconds really is.

Screens

With another player—even a backup goalie—setting a screen, your coach or a trusted shooter shoots low shots toward you, utilizing the screen. It's to the coach's advantage to shoot these himself as he will be able to tell when you were or weren't screened. Always schedule screen shot practice for a few minutes *after* completion of the warmup.

WARMUP

Coaches, *who* warms up your goalie is just as important as how they go about it. Only you or your most trusted players who are properly instructed should be allowed to warm up your goalies.

The first thing to remember to warm your goalie properly is rarely to shoot on goal as hard as you can. Your goalie will see plenty of hard shots in the course of practice and the warmup should prepare him for that. The warmup is a *very individual thing* and will vary for different goaltenders. It should never take any longer than 20 minutes, as any work after that is no longer a warmup.

On game day, the warmup should start with your goalie receiving high shots, then shots around the hip area, then bounce shots, and finally a few minutes of shots in different areas. It's also good to get a few shots from feeds, but during a warmup, screens are not necessary. Again, don't shoot too hard!

COMMON ERRORS

There are a few fundamental areas of emphasis that you as coach should continuously stress with your goalie. You must constantly scrutinize your goalie's body and stick positions. Make sure your goalie moves on a constant arc and never gets too close (flat) to the cage.

Your goalie's step technique is also extremely important. Balance is a key; the goalie's feet should never be brought together. Goalies, avoid clicking your heels together. Step at the ball, and not at the shooter. Any false step, or stutter step backward, must be corrected as soon as possible. Hopping or jumping at the ball can lead to twisting the stick as well as the body.

TIPS, SUGGESTIONS, TRAINING AIDS

There are a few training aids that you, as a goalie, can use to help prepare yourself. Jumping rope and playing squash or racquetball are excellent ways to develop quickness and agility. A weighted or heavy stick can help develop your upper body strength and hand speed.

As a goalie, you should receive all types of shots when going through your warmup. High shots in tight are just as important as long, outside bounce shots. If you're an experienced goalie, you should consider trying to alter your body position in the goal in an attempt to bait shooters to shoot to a certain area. By consciously overplaying to the off-stick side, you can entice shooters to shoot to your stick side.

At key times, you need to make calls in a strong voice. Your "Check" calls must be firm and loud. After possession is secured, "Clear" or "Break" calls must also be emphatic. Finally, you should learn as quickly as possible to accept screens as an occupational hazard, and not overreact.

Coaches and teammates should treat their goalie a special way. Goalies must be encouraged not to dwell on the negative. Coaches and fellow players: Reinforce your goalie's strong points, but never try to make him something he is not.

A big save by a goalie can often inspire a team to higher levels of play.

1. Lead with your hands.
2. Maintain proper distance between your hands.
3. Move efficiently.
4. Be aggressive yet relaxed.
5. Concentrate on the ball.
6. Have good position on the arc.
7. Take the proper step.
8. Keep your elbows loose.
9. Be ready to do anything to stop the ball.
10. Believe you can stop every shot.

11

Face-Offs

The face-off is a specialized, unique skill, and an integral aspect of every lacrosse game. A face-off at the center of the field, usually between the two center midfielders, initiates play at the beginning of each period and after each goal. Possession of the ball is necessary to score; therefore, control of the face-off has a direct bearing on the outcome of every game. Consistent face-off success can allow a good team to dominate, an average team to become good, and a weak team to be competitive. Quick scoring opportunities can develop immediately from the face-off, creating the stuff of exciting, fourth quarter comebacks.

Face-off men must constantly refine the skills and coordination efforts required to gain control of the ball. Quickness, strength, agility, and concentration are the essential requirements of a good face-off man. Although size is certainly an asset, smaller face-off men who are technique-conscious may also be very effective. The face-off is always begun with both players in a right-handed position, although many excellent face-off specialists have been natural left-handers.

Before the referee sounds his whistle to start play, each face-off man must be in proper position. The face-off men stand on the same side of the center line of the field as the goal each is defending. Their sticks rest on the ground along the center line with the pockets in a back-to-back position. Each player *must have both hands on the handle of his own stick and touching the ground.* The players' feet may not touch the sticks, nor may either player be in contact with his opponent's body by encroaching in his opponent's territory. The walls of the two sticks must be approximately one inch apart, so that when the ball is placed between them, it cannot touch the ground. Both hands and both feet of each player must be to the left of the throat of his stick. The left foot must be extended behind the plane of the stick handle. After placing the ball between the sticks, the official sounds his whistle to start play. Each player attempts to direct the course of the ball by stick movement and body position.

A specialized skill and a key factor in the outcome of every lacrosse game, a face-off is like a controlled explosion.

The Face-Off Stance

The coiled body position allows an explosive movement at the sound of the whistle. The wrist of the right hand can be curled under the handle to improve leverage.

Front/back view (A).

Side view (B).

Overhead view (C).

FACE-OFF TECHNIQUES

There are a variety of techniques or face-off moves used to gain control of the ball. We will examine three basic face-off techniques: 1) *the clamp-and-step,* 2) *the push clamp,* and 3) *the rake.* Most face-off men will assume a basic stance and body position regardless of the technique they plan to use. The feet are placed hip width apart. The right foot is even with the right hand and slightly ahead of the left foot. The right hand is placed, palm up, as far up the handle toward the throat as possible. The palm of the left hand is down and can be positioned anywhere from 12 to 18 inches from the right hand. The right elbow is inside the right knee. By starting in a low crouched position and leaning slightly to the right, the face-off man exerts considerable downward pressure on the head of his stick. The wall of the stick should be completely flush with the ground. This starting position is designed for quick explosive movement. Face-off men should neither relax, nor try to get too comfortable in their stance.

The Clamp-and-Step

The clamp-and-step is a traditional power move, the first that most face-off men learn to execute. After assuming the basic face-off stance, you should lean slightly to the right, resting your weight on the right hand, not the right foot.

At the whistle, here's how to execute a coordinated simultaneous clamp-and-step. Staying low, drive your right hand down and pull your left hand toward your left shin, clamping your stick over the ball. The fingers of the right hand rub on the ground while the shoulders and forearms drive into your opponent and attempt to move him off the ball. A short, quick step with your right foot to the head of your stick will provide power for the clamp. This step will also put your body in proper position to turn your backside into your opponent and box him out.

Once you have clamped successfully, it may be necessary to pivot in a circle, keeping the ball between your feet, while shielding your opponent from the ball. Stay low, with a wide base, to prevent being pushed off the ball. The final phase of the face-off involves scooping the ball off the ground. It may not always be possible or wise to scoop the ball at your feet. With the ball controlled under your stick, you can push the ball to an open area before attempting to gain control. At other times, it may be advantageous to kick the ball out to an open area, or redirect the ball to a teammate coming in from the wing.

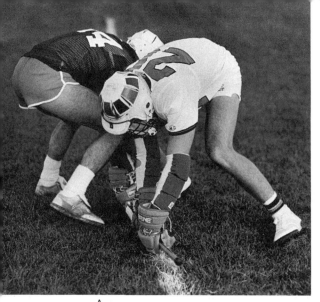

A   B

The Clamp-and-Step

The clamp-and-step is a power face-off move. To perform the maneuver successfully, at the whistle drive your right hand down and your left hand back toward your left shin, clamping the head of your stick over the ball. Simultaneously step forward with your right

The ball can also be pushed forward after the clamp-and-step (A,B).

A   B

C   D

foot and drive your right shoulder into your opponent (A,B). Keep your eye on the ball. Here, the man clamping pushes the ball between his own legs (and away from his opponent) (C), allowing him to pivot free for the scoop (D).

The Push Clamp

The push clamp, a variation of the clamp-and-step, has become very popular in recent years. The stance is basically the same, with perhaps slightly less body lean to the right. The right foot is flat on the ground and the heel of the left foot is up, placing the weight on the toes. You should concentrate on maintaining balanced body position at all times.

The instant the whistle sounds, you must step with the left foot and concentrate on the movement of both hands. The clamping motion of the right hand turns the stick forward and down, reversing the relative positions of the two sidewalls on the stick; that is, the sidewall that started flat on the ground is replaced by the opposite sidewall due to the clamping motion. The left-hand movement is very critical. The handle of the stick is "punched" forward. Rolling the left wrist down and rubbing the left forearm on the ground will ensure that the handle stays as low as possible as it is "punched" forward.

The pivot on the right foot will assist in determining which direction to pull the ball. Care should be taken not to attempt to pick the ball up too soon. The ball can be pulled forward or back, depending on the position of your opponent.

The Push Clamp

At the whistle, the player in white executing the push clamp rolls his stick forward and down with his right hand while simultaneously punching the stick forward with his left (A,B). Throughout its "punch", the left hand is kept low. Once he has clamped the ball (C), the player can decide whether to pull it forward or back for the scoop.

A

The Rake

The rake emphasizes quickness rather than strength and is an excellent counter move to the clamp. The instant the whistle sounds, the center pushes into his opponent's stick and quickly draws his stick to the left. This pulling, or raking, motion should be completed with the stick facing parallel to the midline and pulled directly toward the sideline. To perform the rake successfully, you must concentrate on staying low and keeping the ball in sight. As you push the stick forward and rake it toward the sideline, the ball should catch on the back edge of the head of your stick and roll out to your left, where you can normally scoop it with ease. Successful quick rakes may create fast-break opportunities.

A

The Rake

The rake requires quickness and finesse. As the name implies, the ball is raked quickly to the face-off man's left by a sweeping motion parallel to the midline (A,B). The ball will normally carry beyond the stick where it can be easily scooped (C).

B

C

WING PLAY

Controlling the face-off is a three man proposition. Obviously, the center mid-die is the primary focus. However, he must be supported by well-positioned, alert teammates coming off the wings.

The wing midfielder to the face-off man's right (M_3) provides defensive support. He will normally align along the wing area line on the defensive half of the field. The defensive wing must be alert to cut off the fast break and to provide immediate assistance on ground balls. Wing midfielders must always keep their sticks ready. The ball is the primary concern. The wing area line

B

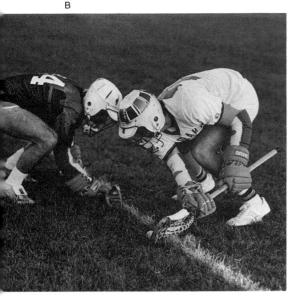

C

Wing play on the face-off.

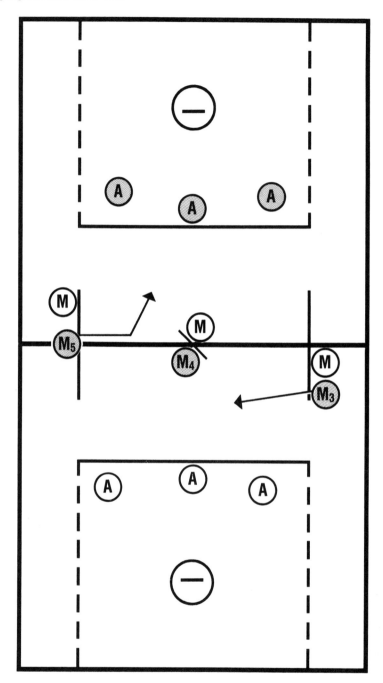

M_3's function is to provide defensive support, cutting off the fast break or providing assistance on ground balls. Depending on the situation, M_5 must be prepared either to receive an outlet pass from M_4 or to assist in scooping a loose ball.

extends 10 yards to either side of the midline, lending plenty of flexibility as to where the defensive wing aligns.

The wing midfielder to the face-off man's left (M_5) has offensive responsibilities. He should align himself in anticipation of where he feels the ball will be directed. As M_5 runs toward the center of the field, he must read the situation. If M_4 can gain control by himself, M_5 must provide a release for a quick pass. M_5 should also be alert to assist M_4 in scooping the loose ball. Communication between M_4 and M_5 is very important. Each must provide ground ball and release support for the other. Their first objective is to gain control of the ball, and then to put as much immediate pressure on the defense as possible.

Following the face-off, the attackmen in the goal area must be alert for two distinct possibilities. If a fast break develops off the face-off, the attack must set up quickly, filling the three predetermined spots. On the other hand, an alert attack may be in position to jump the opponent's face-off middie if he gains control of the ball near the restraining line.

Likewise, the defense must be ready to drop into their fast-break defensive triangle immediately following a face-off. They also can assist their face-off man by providing a release if necessary.

FACE-OFF MAXIMS

1. Anticipate the whistle, explode, stay low, and keep your eyes on the ball. Concentrate on technique.

2. Foot placement of the stance is an individual preference. Balance, not comfort, is necessary for a good stance.

3. Use your hips and backside to move your opponent off the ball.

4. Work hard to develop upper body strength. Talk to your coach or gym teacher about an appropriate strength program for you, and see *Sports Illustrated Strength Training,* by John Garhammer (*Sports Illustrated Winner's Circle Books,* 1987) as a useful reference.

5. Whenever possible, scoop the ball with two hands on your stick.

6. Communication between the face-off man and his teammates on the wings is essential.

7. Do not attempt to scoop the ball too soon. Get your body in position and push or kick the ball to an open area.

8. Be ready to pass immediately after gaining control of the ball.

9. Do not be too predictable. Master one technique, but be able to execute counter moves if you are having trouble.

Gaining control of the ball after a face-off is never easy. The man who stays low and under control, with his eye on the ball, will win most of the time.

10. Be quick. Stay balanced. Be aggressive and always persistent.

Every team should have at least three reliable face-off men. They must practice religiously, concentrating on technique and quick reactions. The face-off specialists are in the spotlight every game. Their performance will set the tone for the entire team.

12

Practice: Planning and Organization

Like those for most team sports, lacrosse practices require careful planning and organization. The nature of the game, with its fundamental skills, specialized techniques, and coordinated team concepts, places particular emphasis on well designed practice sessions. Lacrosse is a player's game. That is, athletes can enjoy the practices because a fair amount of actual scrimmage work can be built into the workouts. From firsthand experience, I know athletes respond positively to well organized, carefully planned practice sessions.

Well-organized practice sessions move smoothly from one drill to the next. Crisp and enthusiastic execution will result if there is a minimum of standing around. Drills should be organized to allow a maximum number of repetitions, yet not at the expense of proper execution. Proper technique must be emphasized at all times. Nothing is more counter productive than to continuously practice a skill improperly.

If you're a lacrosse coach, a pre-season chart listing all the fundamental skills, team concepts, and special game situations will help you develop a logical teaching progression. Weekly objectives can be organized into daily practice plans by referring to the checklist. Certain individual skills and team concepts on the checklist should be drilled daily. However, there are a few special game situations that require rehearsal far less frequently. The checklist system for practice organization serves as a reminder to you, and also helps to insure proper game preparation. The weekly practice checklist for a college team will obviously differ from that of a developmental or high school program. Solid emphasis on conditioning and fundamental skills should be a focus of all programs.

235

Summer lacrosse camps usually emphasize quality instruction and practice.

A Typical Practice Checklist

PRACTICE CHECKLIST	N.	TUES.	WED.	THURS	FRI.
FUNDAMENTAL SKILLS					
Passing/Catching					
Scooping					
Dodging					
Shooting					
Checking					
Footwork/Agility					
SPECIALIZED SKILLS					
Goalie Warmup					
Face-Off					
Cutting-Feeding					
TEAM CONCEPTS					
Riding					
Clearing					
3-Man Plays (A & M)*					
Team Offense					
Team Defense					
Fast Break (Off.)					
Fast Break (Def.)					
Slow Break (Off.)					
Slow Break (Def.)					
EMO-MDD					
SPECIAL GAME SITUATIONS					
MDD Clear					
EMO Ride					
Short Time Play					
Delay Offense					
Mayday Defense					
Shut-Off (EMO & MDD)					
EMO (F/O)**					
MDD (F/O)**					

*A&M—Attackers & Midfielders
**F/O—Full Offense

Weekly practice objectives and daily practice plans can all originate from the checklist.

DAILY PRACTICE SCHEDULE

A high school or college lacrosse team will normally practice between an hour and a half to two hours per day. Early in the season, as new drills and offensive schemes are implemented, full two-hour workouts may be necessary. Arranging the practice sessions into separate segments will help to make optimum use of the allotted times.

The Individual Period

At Hobart, where I coach, we normally start practice with a 15 minute *Individual Period.* This is an informal pre-practice time which allows players to isolate and improve skills that do not get enough attention once formal practice begins. Our attackmen and midfielders make good use of this L.I.P. (Lacrosse Improvement Period) to work hard on their shooting. The attack and midfield can work together in a cutting and feeding drill, or they work on separate goals, concentrating on three-man-plays. The emphasis is on a volume of shots. Quite often we will string a 5 ft $\times$ 5 ft shooting net in the goal during these sessions. The net is suspended in the face of the goal and only allows shots to score that are directed at the corners, along the pipes, or down along the ground. This device helps teach players to shoot for a spot.

Individual Period also provides the goalies with an opportunity to get a thorough warmup. A concentrated warmup, complete with feeds, screens, and outlet passes, will prepare your goalies for any live drills scheduled for later in practice. Face-off men can take advantage of this period to work on their form, whistle reaction, moves and counter-moves. Defensemen can make good use of the *Individual Period* to work on long passes, backhand passes, or loose ball play at the midline.

Since our formal warmup and stretch follows the *Individual Period,* we stay away from any strenuous drills that require quick changes of direction. The atmosphere is relaxed during this pre-practice session. In addition to some good natured kidding, the coaches and players will use this time to exchange thoughts on match-ups and strategy against the upcoming opponent.

The Warmup and Stretch Period

Formal practice begins with a few laps around the field, followed by a 10-minute team *Warmup and Stretch Period.* The primary purpose of this time segment is to physically prepare everyone for practice. The emphasis is on maintaining

Two Basic Agility Drills

A

B

C

The shuffle drill.
In this drill, players stand in a line and practice moving laterally to either side. The players here show excellent shuffle technique: a wide stance, forward body lean, and elevated stick position.

A   B   C

The down-the-line agility drill.
In this drill, the player runs forward while maintaining constant eye contact (with a coach, ballcarrier, teammate, etc.) over either shoulder. Note the succinct pivoting technique.

muscle tone and flexibility, using calisthenics and stretching exercises. The players must be periodically reminded to use this time wisely and to get thoroughly stretched out and ready to practice. A quick set of agility drills follows the team stretch, and then we are ready to go to work.

The Fundamental Skills Period

A 15- to 20-minute *Fundamental Skills Period* normally follows the team warmup and stretch. Stickwork drills that emphasize catching, throwing, dodging, and scooping should be implemented at this time. Changing the drills periodically will help to prevent boredom and keep the players alert. Concentration, communication, and intensity should be stressed during these drills.

Five Basic Stickwork Drills

Triangle catch.
Players should be sure to stay wide when working in triangles. The ball is always passed and received with the stick to the outside. Never bring the stick across your face. Always pivot away from the center of the triangle, change hands on your stick, then execute the pass on the move.

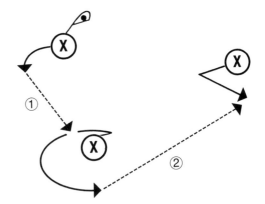

The diamond drill.
This drill is executed all right-handed, then all left. The ball moves quickly around the diamond. X_1 passes to X_2 and runs to the opposite line. X_2 passes to X_3, who quickly passes to X_4. X_3 continues to the opposite line as well. X_2 and X_4 always remain on the points of the diamond. The other players exchange places after passing.

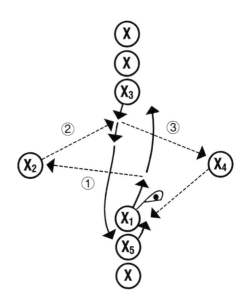

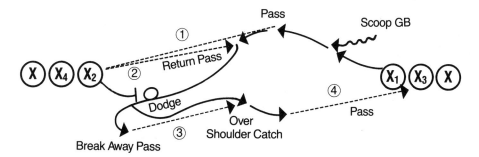

The "S" drill.

This drill looks more involved than it really is. X_1 begins by scooping a ground ball. He passes to X_2, who immediately passes the ball back to X_1. X_1 then executes a predetermined dodge on X_2. X_2 then breaks across the field, looking to receive a pass over the shoulder. After catching the pass from X_1, X_2 passes to X_3, who rolls the ball out for himself, repeating the sequence with the next player in line, X_4.

The 3-man weave.

This excellent conditioner drills the concept of keeping the ball moving upfield. X_1 passes to X_2, then hustles behind X_2 and upfield. X_2 passes to X_3 moving upfield, then folds in behind him. X_3 looks to pass to X_1, who by now should be up ahead of the ball. All passes should be made upfield with the stick in the hand nearest the sideline.

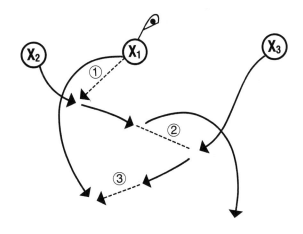

The 3-man vision.

This drill follows the same concept as the weave, but now the players move straight down the field. X_1 should change hands on his stick as he passes to either X_2 or X_3, both of whom should always pass back to X_1 with their stick in the hand nearest the sideline.

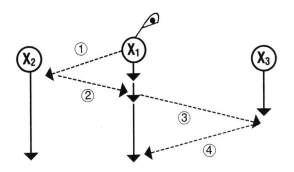

Players should always hustle from one drill to the next.

Stickwork drills should always be executed on the move. Younger players need to be frequently reminded not to save steps. Coaches should be sure to allow adequate time for stickwork drills to be executed right-handed and left-handed. To get the most out of these fundamental stickwork drills, the players should stay spread, throwing at least 15 to 20 yard passes. Traditional stickwork drills place players in two lines with three to four players in each line. Triangle stickwork drills with three players in a line create different passing angles and provide a change of pace for the players.

Two Basic Groundball Drills

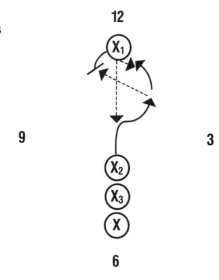

Clock ground balls.

In this drill, ground balls are scooped from one of four predetermined angles corresponding to the positions on a clock (here, the choreography for the 12 o'clock position is diagrammed). X_1 rolls the ball to X_2. X_2 scoops the ground ball and passes to X_1. X_1 returns the ball to X_2, who is now positioned at 12 o'clock. X_2 then rolls the ball out for X_3. X_1 returns to the end of the line.

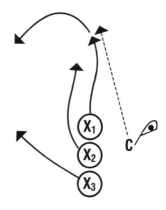

Pressure release.

Here, the coach rolls the ball out for X_1. X_2 chases and attempts to check X_1's back hand as X_1 scoops the ball. X_3 pops out and provides a release for X_1, who makes a wide, arcing turn before attempting to pass.

Defensive Stickwork on the Pressure Release Drill

A

The defender (here, in white) chases while his opponent scoops the loose ball (A). The defender's objective: to cause a turnover by checking the opponent's back hand (B,C).

B

C

The Team Period

Concentrated teaching and game preparation follows the *Fundamental Skills* period. The pace of practice slows during *Team Period* as coaches and players work together on team offensive patterns and team defensive slides. The length of this segment of practice will vary with the age and skill level of the athletes. "Keep it simple" is definitely a rule to follow when coaching players 14 years of age and under. Younger athletes will have a difficult time understanding and executing anything but the most basic offenses. Too much time spent standing and explaining will dampen their enthusiasm. Remember, lacrosse is a player's game, so keep it short and simple when working with younger players.

Three Full-Field Team Period Drills

The full-field clear, 8 lines.

This is a good drill for improving goalie release passes and full-field clearing. The goalie, G1, passes to X_1, who runs a "banana route" upfield and toward the sideline. X_1 passes to X_2 breaking down to receive the ball. X_2 passes to X_3 breaking upfield. X_3 makes a long diagonal pass to X_4. X_4 receives the lobbed ball on the run, passes across the front of the goal mouth to X_5, who tosses the ball to the other goalie, G2. Now G2 starts the drill up the other sideline.

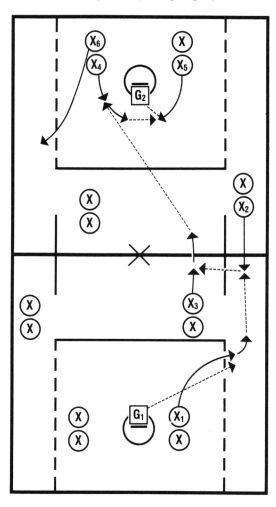

Team Period is often organized six on six, with the field divided in half. By working on two half fields simultaneously, more players are kept active and the offensive and defensive teaching groups can be kept separate. Controlled, half-field scrimmages can be scheduled at this time as well as concentrated work on Extra-Man-Offense and Man-Down-Defense. Three versus three unit face-off practice for the midfielders can also be worked into this time slot, and there is plenty of opportunity for one-on-one instruction during this part of practice, too. The Team Period format facilitates pulling players aside individually or in small groups to offer suggestions and coaching points.

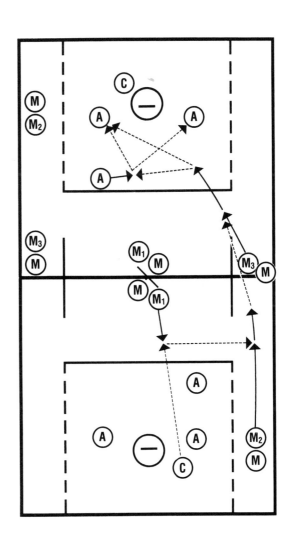

The full-field clear, skeleton fast break.

In this fast-paced drill, the coach, positioned behind the goal, rolls the ball down the middle of the field. The midfielder, M_1, comes down from the face-off "X," scoops the ground ball, and passes quickly to the sideline. The midfielder, M_2, breaking up the sideline, receives the ball and quickly passes to M_3 breaking over the midline. M_3 carries the ball down the field and executes a skeleton fast break *up* the field with the attack. All the middies go to the line to which they passed. The last middie down the field, M_3, must go to the midfield "X" to keep the lines even.

Three Full-Field Team Period Drills (Cont.)

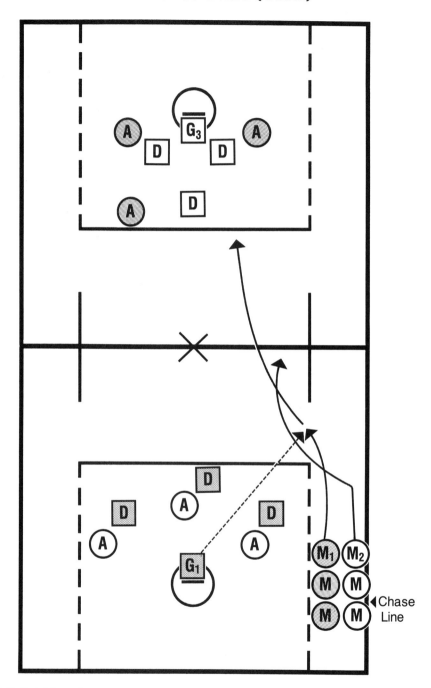

A live full-field fast break with a chaser.
Here, the middie, M_1, in the left line breaks out and receives a pass from the goalie, G1. M_2 pauses, then chases M_1 downfield. M_1 executes a 4 versus 3 with the attack which is already positioned at the far goal (A).

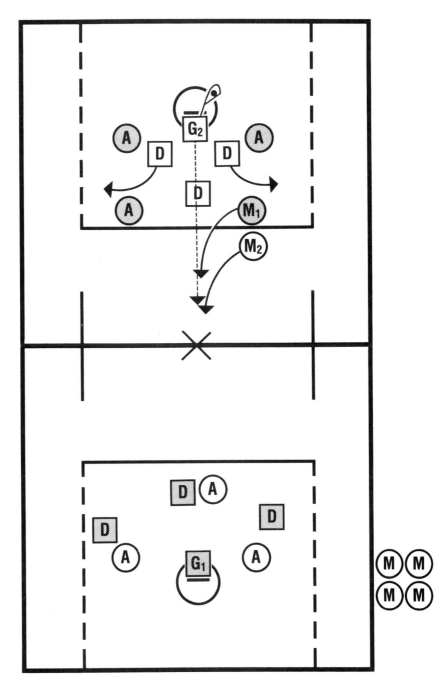

After a shot, save, or goal, G2 quickly grabs a ball and looks to pass to M_2 breaking back upfield. M_1 hustles back into the hole, trying to beat the ball downfield and prevent the fast break (B).

Scrimmage Period

The half-field concepts stressed in the *Team Period* provide a solid foundation for the full-field *Scrimmage Period.* The pace and intensity of practice increases as the players concentrate on riding, clearing, the transition game, and special game situations. *Scrimmage Period* is definitely up tempo, and coaching points are made off to the side as the players focus on execution and hustling on the field.

The sense of urgency and intensity created during this part of practice is excellent preparation for pressure game situations. Throughout the *Scrimmage Period,* coaches should stress the tremendous importance of communication between players. All successful lacrosse teams share at least one common quality: They talk and listen to one another effectively.

Conditioning is a major concern for coaches as they prepare their teams for the physical demands of lacrosse. Players should be encouraged to take part, during the off season, in weight training with an emphasis on improving upper body strength. Wrist rolls are excellent for developing wrist and forearm strength that will enhance shot velocity and checking power. These should be done in season as well as out of season.

Wrist Rolls

Daily use of a wrist-roll device can help increase both your shot velocity and checking power.

As much as possible during the season, we try to condition our players within the structure of practice. Conditioning at the end of practice takes time away from the workout and is often perceived as punishment. Instead, we try to utilize drills within the practice structure that require the players to run hard and push themselves physically, while developing a lacrosse skill.

Lacrosse players will respond to whatever you as a coach stress with sincerity and enthusiasm. We can achieve many of our conditioning goals by encouraging players to hustle and run hard during the drills. Full-field, three-man weave and vision-stickwork drills are excellent conditioners and skill developers.

There will be times when post practice conditioning must be planned to gain that extra edge. Pyramid sprints can be an effective conditioner. Starting on the endline, the players sprint to the GLE and back, then to the restraining line and back, and finally to the midline and back. As a change of pace at the end of practice we occasionally run a ground ball "inning drill." The players align in groups of three, facing one another on either restraining line. The first player in each line scoops a ground ball and sprints 40 yards to the far restraining line, placing the ball down. The next man in line then repeats the scoop and the 40 yard sprint. One inning elapses when each player has made one scoop and sprint. Coaches control the conditioning by requiring five, seven, nine, or "extra innings." Occasionally, we will concentrate on endurance and make the sprints 220s. Starting on one sideline at the GLE, the players run in groups by position to the far GLE, around the goal, and back along the far sideline.

Whenever possible, we like to end practice on a positive note. Bringing the team together to share an amusing anecdote or to single out one player for some good natured kidding helps to build unity, and an eagerness to return to practice the next day.

CLOSING WORDS

As we have seen, a stick, a ball, a wall, and a little imagination are all that you need to start building a solid fundamental foundation of lacrosse skills. Thereafter, watching top college or club lacrosse teams at play is an excellent way to learn how to apply those fundamentals within the structure of team offense and defense. Once you have those skills down and can begin to apply them in game situations, watch out: Lacrosse is an addictive sport, and its pleasures can

Two of the many possible rewards of lacrosse: a National Collegiate Championship plaque, and the satisfaction of having played your best on a winning team.

be enjoyed at any level of play. Furthermore, as you continue to grow with the game, your enjoyment of it grows, too.

Along with my livelihood as a coach, I owe lacrosse a wealth of wonderful experiences and friendships. May this book help unlock the door to such experiences and friendships for you.

Play well. Give back. And enjoy.

Glossary

Arc: The semicircular path between the two goal pipes that goalies position themselves on.

Attackmen: The three offensive players that operate around the goal area.

Backup: An off-ball defender in position to support a teammate guarding an opponent with the ball.

Ball stop: A piece of foam rubber that adheres to the throat of the stick and facilitates holding the ball in the pocket.

Body check: A deliberate bumping of an opponent from the front—above the knees and below the neck—when the opponent is in possession or within five yards of the ball.

Bull dodge: To drive past a defender, using speed and power.

Butt: The lower end of the handle of the stick.

Butt-end hold: A method of applying defensive pressure when playing stick-on-stick in which the defender places his fists on an opponent's upper arm or shoulder and with his stick in a vertical position.

Catching: Receiving a pass in your stick.

Change-of-direction dodge: A series of zigzag maneuvers alternating both body direction and the position of the hands on the stick.

Checking: Attempting to dislodge the ball from your opponent's stick.

Check-up: A call given by the goalie to tell each defender to find his man and call out his opponent's number.

Clamp: A face-off maneuver executed by quickly pushing the back of your stick over on top of the ball.

Clear: Running or passing the ball from the defensive half of the field to the attack goal area.

Close defense: The three defensive players that work in coordination with the goalie to prevent the opponent from scoring.

Cradling: The rhythmical coordinated motion of the arms and wrists that keeps the ball secure in the stick and ready to be passed or shot.

Crease: The circle with a nine-foot radius around each goal.

Cross check: An illegal check or hold using the area of the stick handle between the hands.

Cross-handed defense: Individual defensive technique where the defenseman maintains a forearm hold on the ballcarrier.

Cutting: A movement by an offensive player without the ball, toward the opposition goal, and in anticipation of a feed and subsequent shot.

Dodges: Ball-carrying maneuvers used for eluding defenders.

Endline: The boundary at opposite ends of the field that runs parallel to the midline.

Extra-man offense (EMO): A one-man advantage (at least) that occurs following a time-serving penalty; normally a six-on-five situation.

Face dodge: A dodge executed by quickly bringing the stick across your face while running at a defender.

Face-off: A one-on-one technique used to put the ball in play to start each period and following each goal.

Fast break: A transition scoring opportunity with the offense enjoying at least a one-man advantage.

Feeding: Passing the ball to a teammate who is in position for a shot on goal.

Forearm hold: A method of applying pressure when playing crosshanded defense in which a defender places his forearm on the opponent's upper arm area with his stick across the chest of the opponent.

Front swing: A maneuver by an individual offensive player where he begins along the goal line extended (GLE) and then quickly swings to the front of the goal.

Goalkeeper: The player whose main responsibility is to stop shots on goal while directing the defense to act as a cohesive unit.

Goal line: The six-foot-long stripe between the goalposts.

Goal line extended (GLE): An imaginary line running parallel to the endlines that runs from the goal to the sideline.

Ground ball: A loose ball anywhere on the playing field. Opposing teams fight for possession using body and stick checks as well as scooping techniques.

Handle: An aluminum or wooden pole connected to the head of a stick; the part of the stick that players grasp when executing any maneuver with their sticks.

Head: The plastic part of the stick connected to the handle.

Holds: See forearm hold and butt-end hold.

Holding: A technical foul committed either by grabbing an opponent or by hindering a ballcarrier's progress with one's stick.

Inbounds play: A planned offensive maneuver designed to create a quick shot after the ball is brought into play from the endline.

Inside roll: A variation of the change of direction roll dodge in which an offensive player, usually an attackman, drives from behind the goal above the GLE and rolls back behind his defender for a shot right on top of the goalie.

Interference: A technical foul committed by preventing the free movement of an opponent who is neither in possession of the ball nor within five yards of a loose ball.

Isolation: An offensive tactic employed in which an area of the field is cleared to allow the ballcarrier to dodge to the goal and go one-on-one against the goalkeeper.

Man-down defense (MDD): The situation that results from a time-serving penalty against the defense in which the defense plays with at least a one-man disadvantage.

Man-to-man defense: A tactic employed in which each defender guards one opponent wherever that opponent moves.

Midfielders: The three players who play in the center of the field and play both offense and defense.

Midline: The line that bisects the field and runs from sideline to sideline.

One-on-one: A situation in which one defender is matched against a ballcarrier. This term may also be used to describe the situation in which a goalkeeper faces an unguarded shooter from a close distance.

Overhand: A method of passing or shooting in which a player, keeping the stick perpendicular to the ground, releases the ball by snapping his top hand straight over the top of his shoulder.

Offside: A technical foul in which the offending team has either fewer than three men in its offensive half of the field or fewer than four men in its defensive half of the field.

Passing: The art of throwing the ball to a teammate.

Pick: An offensive maneuver in which one player attempts to block the path of a defender guarding another offensive player.

Push: A technical foul in which the offending player strikes the opponent from behind.

Poke check: A stick check in which the player thrusts the stick like a pool cue at the opponent through the top hand by pushing with the bottom hand.

Pocket: The strung part of the head of the stick which holds the ball.

Rake: A face-off move in which a player sweeps the ball to a particular area.

Riding: The act of preventing a team from clearing the ball.

Roll dodge: A dodge in which the ballcarrier spins around his opponent while keeping his body between his stick and his opponent.

Shaft: The handle of the stick.

Scoop: The act of picking up a ground ball.

Screen: An offensive tactic in which a player near the crease positions himself so as to block the goalkeeper's view of the ball.

Shooting: The act of throwing the ball toward the goal in an attempt to score.

Sidearm: A method of shooting or passing the ball by holding the stick parallel to the ground and swinging it across one's body.

Sidelines: The two boundaries that run the entire length of the field.

Slap check: A stick check in which a player snaps his wrists to thrust his stick across his opponent's chest.

Slide: A move by a defender to give support to a teammate who has been beaten by his man.

Split dodge: An offensive maneuver in which the dodger runs at a 45 degree angle one way and quickly brings the stick in front of his face and heads at a 45 degree angle the other way.

Stick-on-stick: A method of individual defense in which a defender carries his stick in the opposite hand of his opponent's stick.

Stack: An offensive alignment in which two players stand side-by-side.

Throat: That part of the head of the stick where the plastic meets the handle.

Underhand: A method of shooting or passing the ball which a player executes by dropping his hand on the stick below his hip and follows through as if pitching a softball.

Unsettled situation: Any fast-break opportunity or any situation when the defense is at less than full strength due to a loose ball or broken clear.

Wrap check: A one-handed check in which the defender drops his bottom hand off the stick and swings his stick around his opponent's body to dislodge the ball.

Zone: A team defensive tactic in which each defender guards an area rather than a man.